JUMP
AT HOME
GRADE
1

NEW EDITION

ALSO BY JOHN MIGHTON

The Myth of Ability

The End of Ignorance

JUMP MATH SERIES

JUMP at Home Grade 1

JUMP at Home Grade 2

JUMP at Home Grade 3

JUMP at Home Grade 4

JUMP at Home Grade 5

JUMP at Home Grade 6

JUMP at Home Grade 7

JUMP at Home Grade 8

JUMP AT HOME

GRADE 1

NEW EDITION

Worksheets for the JUMP Math Program

JOHN MIGHTON

ANANSI

This edition published in 2010 by House of Anansi Press Inc.
www.houseofanansi.com

Some of the material in this book has previously been published by JUMP Math.

Every reasonable effort has been made to contact the holders of copyright for materials reproduced in this work. The publishers will gladly receive information that will enable them to rectify any inadvertent errors or omissions in subsequent editions.

21 20 19 18 17   5 6 7 8 9

Library and Archives Canada Cataloguing in Publication

Cataloguing data available from Library and Archives Canada

Library of Congress Control Number: 2010924088

Acknowledgements
Writers: Dr. John Mighton, Dr. Sindi Sabourin, and Dr. Anna Klebanov
Text design: Pam Lostracco
Layout: Rita Camacho, Pam Lostracco, and Ilyana Martinez
Illustrations: Pam Lostracco

This book, like the JUMP program itself, is made possible by the efforts of the volunteers and staff of JUMP Math.

 Canada Council for the Arts **Conseil des Arts du Canada**    ONTARIO ARTS COUNCIL
CONSEIL DES ARTS DE L'ONTARIO
an Ontario government agency
un organisme du gouvernement de l'Ontario

We acknowledge for their financial support of our publishing program the Canada Council for the Arts, the Ontario Arts Council, and the Government of Canada through the Canada Book Fund.

Printed and bound in Canada

Contents

Unit 2: Patterns and Algebra 1

Unit 3: Measurement 1

Unit 4: Probability and Data Management 1

Unit 5: Number Sense 2

Unit 6: Patterns and Algebra 2

Unit 7: Measurement 2

Introduction: About JUMP Math

There is a prevalent myth in our society that people are born with mathematical talent, and others simply do not have the ability to succeed. Recent discoveries in cognitive science are challenging this myth of ability. The brain is not hard-wired, but continues to change and develop throughout life. Steady, incremental learning can result in the emergence of new abilities.

The carefully designed mathematics in the JUMP Math program provide the necessary skills and knowledge to give your child the joy of success in mathematics. Through step-by-step learning, students celebrate success with every question, thereby increasing achievement and reducing math anxiety.

John Mighton: Founder of JUMP Math

"Nine years ago I was looking for a way to give something back to my local community. It occurred to me that I should try to help kids who needed help with math. Mathematicians don't always make the best teachers because mathematics has become obvious to them; they can have trouble seeing why their students are having trouble. But because I had struggled with math myself, I wasn't inclined to blame my students if they couldn't move forward."
— John Mighton, *The End of Ignorance*

JUMP Math, a national charity dedicated to improving mathematical literacy, was founded by John Mighton, a mathematician, bestselling author, and award-winning playwright. The organization grew out of John's work with a core group of volunteers in a "tutoring club"; their goal was to meet the needs of the most challenged students from local schools. Over the next three years John developed the early material — simple handouts for the tutors to use during their one-on-one teaching sessions with individual students. This period was one of experimentation in developing the JUMP Math method. Eventually, John began to work in local inner-city schools, by placing tutors in the classrooms. This led to the next period of innovation: using the JUMP Math method on small groups of students.

Teachers responded enthusiastically to the success they saw in their students and wanted to adapt the method for classroom use. In response, the needs of the teachers for curriculum-based resources were met by the development of workbooks. These started out as a series of three remedial books with limited accompanying teacher materials, released in fall 2003. The effectiveness of these workbooks led quickly to the development of grade-specific, curriculum-based workbooks. The grade-specific books were first released in 2004. Around that time, the power of teacher networks in creating learning communities was beginning to take shape.

Inspired by the work he has done with thousands of students over the past twenty years, John has systematically developed an approach to teaching mathematics that is based on fostering brain plasticity and emergent intelligence, and on the idea that children have more potential in mathematics than is generally believed. Linking new research in cognitive science to his extensive observations of students, John calls for a re-examination of the assumptions that underlie current methods of teaching mathematics.

JUMP Math, as a program and as an organization, developed in response to the needs of the students, teachers, schools, and communities where John and the volunteers were working. Recognizing the potential of all students to succeed in mathematics, and to succeed in school, was the motivation that John needed to dedicate more than ten years of his life developing a mathematics program that achieved his vision.

JUMP Math: An Innovative Approach

In only ten years, JUMP Math has gone from John's kitchen table to a thriving organization reaching more than 50,000 students with high-quality learning resources and training for 2,000 teachers. It continues to work with community organizations to reach struggling students through homework clubs and after-school programs. Through the generous support of our sponsors, JUMP Math donates resources to classrooms and homework clubs across Canada. The organization has also inspired thousands of community volunteers and teachers to donate their time as tutors, mentors, and trainers.

JUMP Math is unique; it builds on the belief that every child can be successful at mathematics by

• Promoting positive learning environments and building confidence through praise and encouragement;
• Maintaining a balanced approach to mathematics by concurrently addressing conceptual and procedural learning;
• Achieving understanding and mastery by breaking mathematics down into small sequential steps;
• Keeping all students engaged and attentive by "raising the bar" incrementally; and,
• Guiding students strategically to explore and discover the beauty of mathematics.

JUMP Math recognizes the importance of reducing math anxiety. Research in psychology has shown that our brains are extremely fallible: our working memories are poor, we are easily overwhelmed by too much new information, and we require a good deal of practice to consolidate skills and concepts. These mental challenges are compounded when we are anxious. The JUMP approach has been shown to reduce math anxiety significantly.

JUMP Math scaffolds mathematical concepts rigorously and completely. The materials were designed by a team of mathematicians and educators who have a deep understanding of and a love for mathematics. Concepts are introduced in rigorous steps, and prerequisite skills are included in the lesson. Breaking down concepts and skills into steps is often necessary even with the more able students. Math is a subject in which a gifted student can become a struggling student almost overnight, because mathematical knowledge is cumulative.

Consistent with emerging brain research, JUMP Math provides materials and methods that minimize differences between students, allowing teachers, tutors, and parents to more effectively improve student performance in mathematics. Today, parents have access to this unique innovation in mathematics learning with the revised JUMP at Home books.

JUMP Math at Home

JUMP at Home has been developed by mathematicians and educators to complement the mathematics curriculum that your child learns at school. Each grade covers core skills and knowledge to help your child succeed in mathematics. The program focuses on building number sense, pattern recognition, and foundations for algebra.

JUMP at Home is designed to boost every student's confidence, skills, and knowledge. Struggling students will benefit from practice in small steps, while good students will be provided with new ways to understand concepts that will help them enjoy mathematics even more and to exceed their own expectations.

JUMP Math in Schools

JUMP Math also publishes full curriculum-based resources — including student workbooks, teacher guides with daily lesson plans, and blackline masters — that cover all of the Ontario and the Western Canada mathematics curriculum. For more information, please visit the JUMP Math website, www.jumpmath.org, to find out how to order.

Evidence that JUMP Math Works

JUMP Math is a leader in promoting third-party research about its work. A recent study by researchers at the Ontario Institute for Studies in Education (OISE), the University of Toronto, and Simon Fraser University found that in JUMP Math classrooms conceptual understanding improved significantly for weaker students. In Lambeth, England, researchers reported that after using JUMP Math for one year, 69 percent of students who were two years behind were assessed at grade level.

Cognitive scientists from The Hospital for Sick Children in Toronto recently conducted a randomized-controlled study of the effectiveness of the JUMP math program. Studies of such scientific rigour remain relatively rare in mathematics education research in North America. The results showed that students who received JUMP instruction outperformed students who received the methods of instruction their teachers would normally use, on well-established measures of math achievement.

Using JUMP at Home

"In the twenty years that I have been teaching mathematics to children, I have never met an educator who would say that students who lack confidence in their intellectual or academic abilities are likely to do well in school. JUMP Math has been carefully designed to boost confidence. It has proven to be an extremely effective approach for convincing even the most challenged student that they can do well in mathematics." — John Mighton

Helping your child discover the joy of mathematics can be fun and productive. You are not the teacher but the tutor. When having fun with mathematics, remember the JUMP Math T.U.T.O.R. principles:

Take responsibility for learning:
   If your child doesn't understand a concept, it can always be clarified further or explained differently. As the adult, you are responsible for helping your child understand. If they don't get it, don't get frustrated — get creative!

Use positive reinforcement:
   Children like to be rewarded when they succeed. Praise and encouragement build excitement and foster an appetite for learning. The more confidence a student has, the more likely they are to be engaged.

Take small steps:
   In mathematics, it is always possible to make something easier. Always use the JUMP Math worksheets to break down the question into a series of small steps. Practice, practice, practice!

Only indicate correct answers:
   Your child's confidence can be shaken by a lack of success. Place checkmarks for correct answers, then revisit questions that your child is having difficulty with. Never use Xs!

Raise the bar:
   When your child has mastered a particular concept, challenge them by posing a question that is slightly more difficult. As your child meets these small challenges, you will see their focus and excitement increase.

   And remember: if your child is falling behind, teach the number facts! It is a serious mistake to think that students who don't know their number facts can always get by in mathematics using a calculator or other aids. Students can certainly perform operations on a calculator, but they cannot begin to solve problems if they lack a sense of numbers. Students need to be able to see patterns in numbers, and to make estimates and predictions about numbers, in order to have any success in mathematics. We have put together some fun activities to help you and your child get ready for mathematics!

Counting Backwards

In mathematics, it is important for your child to learn how to count backwards. Many children find counting backwards much more difficult than counting forwards. Here are some things you can do to help your child learn and practice this skill.

Keep Score . . . Backwards!

Count backwards every time you make a catch or hit a ball when you play games such as ping-pong or catch. Start at 5, 10, or 20, and play until you reach 0. Did someone drop or miss the ball? Don't start counting back from the last number — add 3 first! For example, if someone misses the ball at 11, start counting back again from 14. (Your child knows how to add 3, so let him/her do it!)

Count Down the Time

Next time you use a timer around the house (e.g., to microwave popcorn), tell your child how you know when the time is almost up. Watch and chant the last 10 or 20 seconds of the countdown together.

Play Plus or Minus 1

(Game adapted from *Card Games for Smart Kids* by Dr. Margie Golick.)

You will need one deck of cards. Start by removing all of the face cards (King, Queen, Jack) from the deck.

Goal: To place all 40 cards into a new pile

To play:

1. Put the deck face down and turn over the top card. What number is it? Start a new pile with this card.
2. Turn over the next card. What number is it? If it is **1 more or 1 less** than the last card, add it to the pile. Otherwise, put it in another pile (the discard pile).
3. Keep turning cards over and putting them in the appropriate piles until the deck runs out. Then repeat with the cards in the discard pile (and start a new discard pile).
4. Keep playing with the cards in the discard pile. Eventually, you will have placed all the cards into the new pile (and you win!) or you will have some cards left over.

Variation:

Play Plus or Minus 2: Cards go into the new pile if they are **2 more or 2 less** than the last card drawn.

Wait or Go?

Some pedestrian traffic signals include a countdown. If you see such a signal, point out to your child when the countdown starts. Have your child watch the countdown and count backwards with it. Discuss how the countdown helps pedestrians cross the street safely. How do the lights change when the number reaches 0? How does knowing that 9 is far from 0, but 2 is close to 0 help you decide if you have enough time to cross the street or if you should wait?

Sorting

In mathematics, it is important for your child to learn how to sort things into groups. Here are some things you can do together to help your child practice sorting.

Sort laundry

Ask your child to help you sort the laundry into different groups, such as
- shirts, pants, socks
- dark clothes, light clothes
- your clothes, my clothes

Discuss with your child how all of the items in a group are the same and how the groups differ. Can your child think of another way to sort the laundry?

Sort Grocery Items

Ask your child to help you sort grocery items into groups, such as
- dairy products, meat products, other
- things we store in the fridge, things we don't store in the fridge
- things we eat, things we don't eat (e.g., tissues, cat litter, soap)

You can also sort by shape or colour. Can your child think of another way to sort the items?

Sort Cutlery

Ask your child to sort cutlery before putting it away. What groups did your child create? Ask your child to explain why he/she sorted the items that way.

Sort Toys, Books, and Games

Ask your child to sort toys, books, and games before putting them away. If your child's toys are already sorted (e.g., books in a bookcase, games in a box), ask your child to describe how they are sorted. Which items are grouped together? How many groups are there?

How Are Items Sorted?

Look for examples of sorting everywhere you go: at the grocery store, in the library, in stores and shops. Discuss how the items on a shelf or in an aisle are sorted and why they might be sorted that way. For example,

- shoes in a shoe store are often sorted first by age and gender (men, women, kids) and then by type (dress shoes, running shoes, boots, and so on);
- flowers in a flower shop are sorted by type (carnations, lilies, roses) and then sometimes by colour; and
- books at the library or in a bookstore are sorted by subject and by age (fiction, cookbooks, children's books, and so on).

Length

In mathematics, your child needs to learn about length. Comparing lengths is something we all do in daily life. Here are some ways you can compare lengths together at home.

Compare Lengths Directly — Socks

Ask your child to help you sort and match socks after washing. Demonstrate comparing two socks of different lengths by lining up the heel-to-toe parts side by side. Ask: Which one is longer? Which one do you think is mine? Sort the remaining socks into two piles, long and short. (This activity will work best if you have many pairs of plain, unpatterned socks or at least two different sizes of the same pattern.) You can finish sorting and matching the socks together. Once you have sorted them by size, match them by colour and pattern.

Compare Lengths Directly and Indirectly — Hands and Feet

Ask your child: Whose hand is bigger — yours or mine? How can we check? Hold your hand up to your child's to compare them. Then compare the length of your hands to the length of your mittens or gloves. Ask: Will my hand fit in your mitten? Will your hand fit in mine? Repeat for feet and socks/shoes.

Now ask: What's longer — your foot or my hand? How can we check? Before comparing them directly, compare your child's shoe or sock to your glove. Ask: Which one is longer? Your child might want to revise his/her answer to the first question. Now line your hand up with your child's foot to compare the lengths directly.

Here's another way to compare the lengths of your hands and feet indirectly: Trace your child's foot onto paper and ask your child to trace your hand onto paper. Cut the two tracings out and place them one on top of the other.

Compare and Order Lengths

Ask relatives or friends who live far away to trace one hand or paint a handprint onto paper and mail it to you. Compare their hands to yours and your child's. Order the hands from longest to shortest. Who has the longest hand? Who has the shortest hand? With older children, use a ruler and measure directly.

Basic Operations

In mathematics, your child needs to know addition, subtraction, and skip counting forwards (e.g., 5, 10, 15, . . .) and backwards (e.g., 10, 8, 6, . . .). If you have stairs in your home, the games below can help your child master these concepts.

To begin, attach numbers to each step, starting with 1 on the first (bottom) step and going up. (Higher numbers are thus higher in space.) Put a 0 on the floor before the first step. You will also need dice for each game.

Games for 1 Player

- **Adding on Stairs.** Model finding 5 + 3: Stand on the step marked 5 and go up 3 steps. Give children a die to roll. If the first roll is 5, they move up 5 steps and say 0 + 5 = 5. If the second roll is 4, they move up 4 steps and say 5 + 4 = 9. Play continues until children reach the top of the stairs. At the end, children will have to roll the exact number needed to land on the top step.
- **Subtracting on Stairs.** Play as above, but start on the top step and move down, e.g., 8 − 3 = 5.
- **Skip Counting by 2s on Stairs.** Children walk up the steps, one at a time, and say every number that their left (or right) foot lands on. Children should start at 0, and take the number of steps determined by the roll of a die. If they roll a 5, they take 5 steps and say either "1, 3, 5" or "0, 2, 4." The goal is to get to the top of the stairs.
- **Skip Counting Back by 2s on Stairs.** Play as above, but start at the top step and move down.

A Cooperative Game for 2–4 Players

This game combines addition and subtraction. Note that players do not play against each other, but instead work as a team. Parents and children can play together.
- **Adding or Subtracting on Stairs.** Players start on predetermined steps (e.g., 0, 5, 10, and 20). Each player rolls the die in turn and moves accordingly. Players can choose whether to move up (add) or down (subtract), but there can never be more than one player on a step at any time, and players cannot move to the bottom (1) or top step once play has begun. Players say the addition or subtraction sentence corresponding to their move (e.g., 8 − 2 = 6) and try to make as many moves as possible as a team before they get stuck. Play again and try to improve. A supervising or participating adult (or older child) can keep track of how many moves were made.

Telling the Time

In mathematics, your child is learning how to tell time. Your child knows that the "short hand" on a clock is called the hour hand. Because it is longer than the hour hand, we call the minute hand "the long hand."

In class, children often talk about what they do when the hour hand is pointing at different numbers. For example; when the hour hand points at the 10, we go outside for recess. When the hour hand points at the 3, we know that school is almost over.

Here are some ways you can talk about time at home. You will need an analogue clock (a clock with hands).

What Would You Be Doing If . . .

At different times on the weekend, ask your child what he or she would be doing if this were a school day. Emphasize the position of the hour hand each time.

Where Is the Short Hand? What Will We Do?

Ask your child where the short hand is pointing at different times during the day, such as at mealtimes or other regularly scheduled activities (e.g., lessons, visits to friends or family). Then do the reverse: Point out the position of the short hand and ask your child to identify the activity. If you eat supper around 6 p.m., you might say: The short hand is close to the 6. What will we be doing soon?

It's Time For . . .

Identify events that happen at the same time every day or week. For example, if your child has a favourite television show, point out where the short hand is when the show starts. Ask: Is the show on at the same time every day? Every Saturday? How could we check? (Check that channel every day at the same time for a week and record the answers in a chart.)

Changes in Time

Investigate natural events that change predictably over time. Record the times of the events daily or weekly for a few weeks (or more!). Then look for patterns. For example:

*   What time does it get dark outside?
*   How do shadows change? Find a landmark or familiar object near your home that is sometimes in the shade and sometimes in the light. What time does it come into or out of the shade?

"Children will never fulfill their extraordinary potential until we remember how it felt to have so much potential ourselves. There was nothing we weren't inspired to look at or hold, or that we weren't determined to find out how to do. Open the door to the world of mathematics so your child can pass through." — John Mighton

Games, Activities, and Puzzles:
Notes on Games and Activities

Make your own Mindsweeper game.

For this game, you will need a copy of the activity page *Blank Mindsweeper Grids* on page xx. To prepare to play "Mindsweeper," start by filling in four stars in the blank 4 x 4 grid, or five stars in the blank 5 x 5 grid. You may arrange the stars in any way you want. Then, in each non-starred square, write the number of starred squares that it is touching. Two examples, with a 4 x 4 grid filled in, are shown below.

2	*	3	1
2	*	3	*
1	1	3	2
0	0	1	*

2	*	2	*
*	3	3	2
2	3	*	1
*	2	1	1

Cover the squares on the grid with coins about the size of a penny. To play the game, the player removes coins from the squares one at a time. The player may decide to stop removing coins at any time. The player then counts how many starred squares are still covered by coins and how many numbered squares remain covered. The player wins if there are more starred squares still covered than numbered squares covered.

Note: This game is slightly different than the traditional form of the Minesweeper video game. In the traditional game, the player tries to remove all the pennies from the numbered squares, but loses if he or she uncovers any starred square. The Mindsweeper grids can also be used to play the traditional game.

Food Sale

Use the activity page *Food Sale*. You or your child could cut out the receipts. You can take turns being the cashier and the customer. The cashier writes out the receipts for the customer. Each customer is given 5 dimes and should buy as much as they can for their 50¢.

Variation: Try to buy a balanced meal for 50¢, one item from each of the four food groups.

Extension: Use a calculator to add the total amount of money spent, and subtract it from 50¢. Is this the amount of money you have left? Discuss whether you could have paid for all the items at the same time instead of separately.

Matching Analogue to Digital
Literature/Cross-Curricular Connection:

Telling Time: How to Tell Time on Digital and Analogue Clocks **by Jules Older**

This book introduces the how and why of analogue and digital time. Read as an introduction to time — matching digital and analogue notations.

The 2-page activity *Matching Analogue to Digital* is provided for a matching game of analogue and digital time. Start by placing the cards face up and have your child remove pairs of matching cards.

After the child becomes comfortable with this, they can turn the cards face down and play Memory. Game rules: Place the cards face down in an array. Flip over two cards. If the cards match (show the same time), take them away. If they do not match, turn them face down and open a different pair of cards. The goal is to remove all of the cards using as few turns as you can.

Adding and Subtracting on Stairs

Play the games Adding on Stairs and Subtracting on Stairs and Adding or Subtracting on Stairs (see JUMP At Home — Introduction for a description of these games). Then have your child do the activities *Adding on Stairs* and *Subtracting on Stairs*.

Adding on Stairs

Liam goes up 3 steps. Where does he end up?

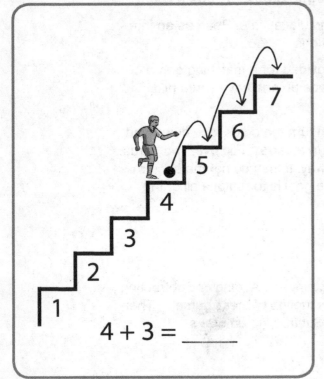

4 + 3 = _____

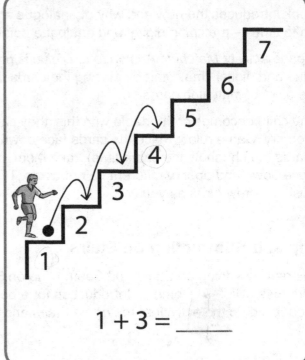

1 + 3 = _____

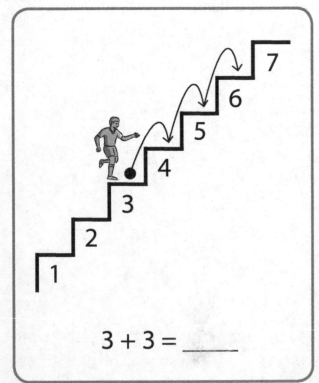

3 + 3 = _____

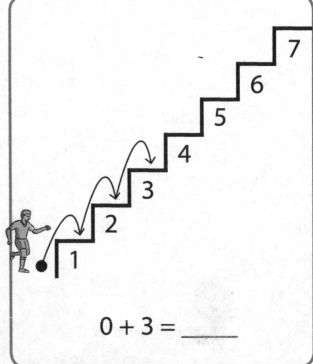

0 + 3 = _____

Adding on Stairs *(continued)*

Count the steps.

Fill in the blanks.

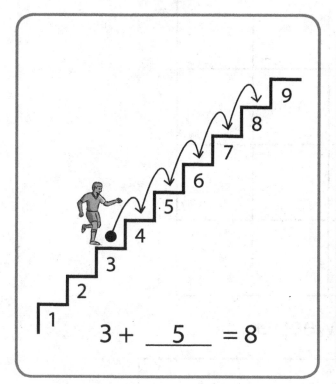

$3 + \underline{\quad 5 \quad} = 8$

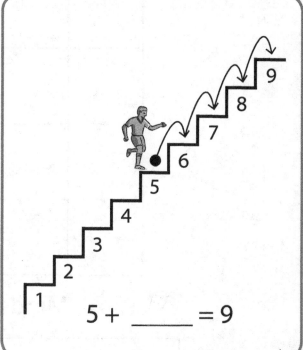

$5 + \underline{\qquad} = 9$

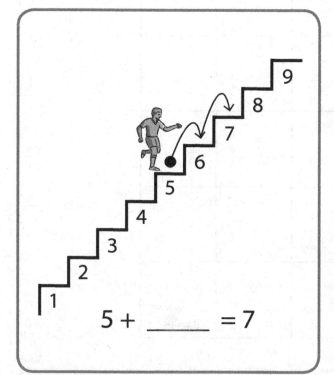

$5 + \underline{\qquad} = 7$

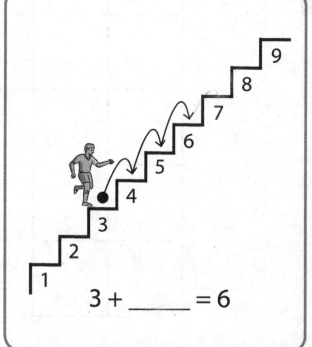

$3 + \underline{\qquad} = 6$

Blank Mindsweeper Grids

Mindsweeper

Mindsweeper

Counting Starred Squares

Colour the squares touching the bold square.

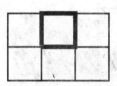 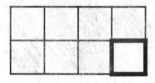 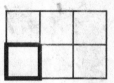 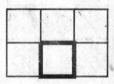

 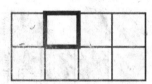 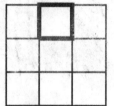 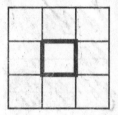

How many starred squares  is the bold square touching?

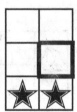 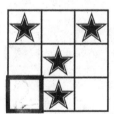 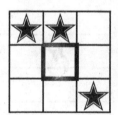

In each square, write how many starred squares it is touching.

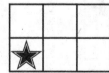 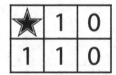 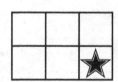

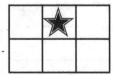 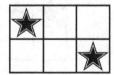 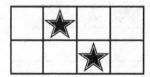

Counting Starred Squares *(continued)*

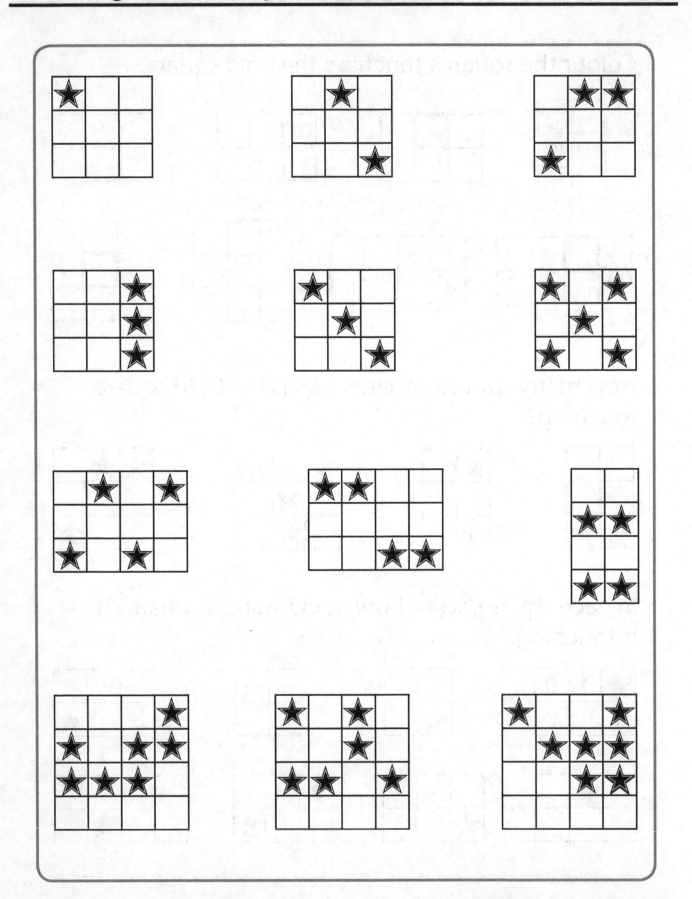

Find the Picture

Colour each part the right colour.

Red adds to 5.
Orange adds to 6.
Green adds to 7.
Yellow adds to 8.

What picture do you see? _____

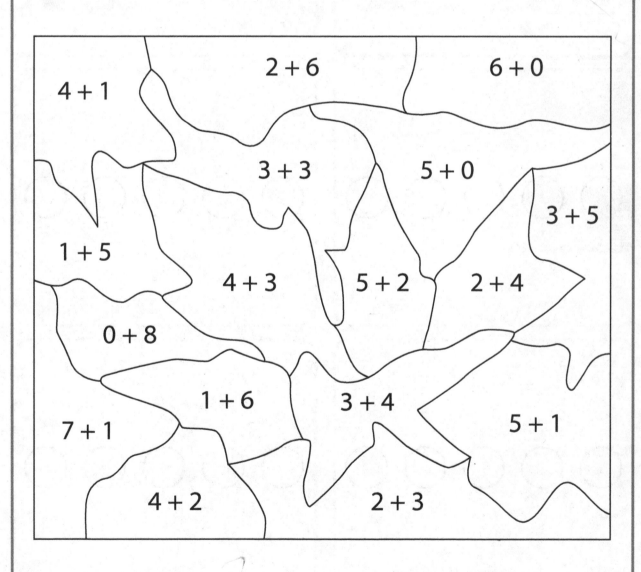

No unauthorized copying   **Games, Activities, and Puzzles**

Many Ways to Colour 3

Challenge: How many ways can you colour 3 different circles?

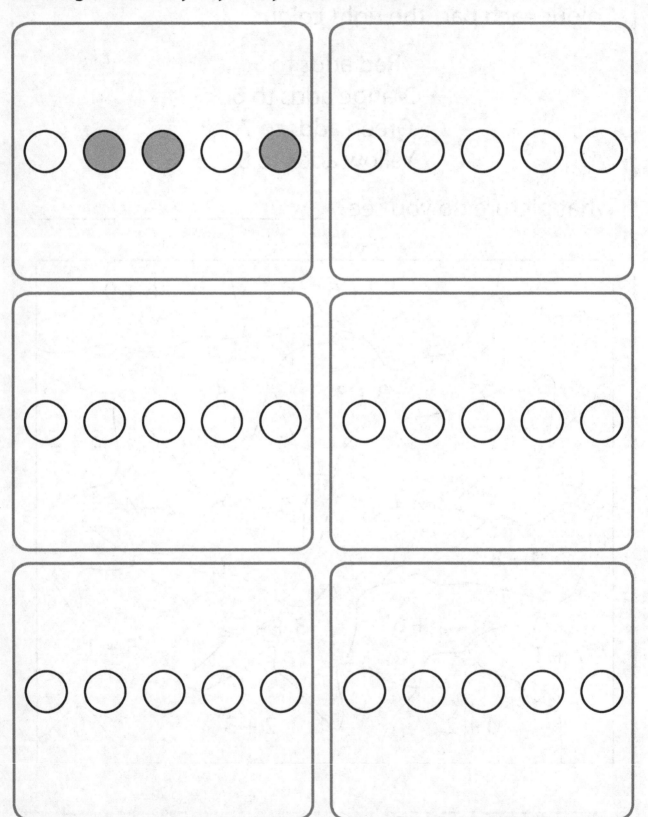

Models of Counting On

Add.

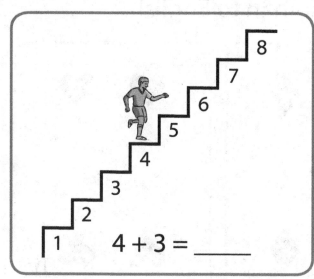

$4 + 3 =$ _____

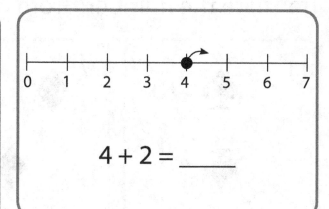

$4 + 2 =$ _____

7

_____   _____
$7 + 1$ $7 + 2$

$7 + 2 =$ _____

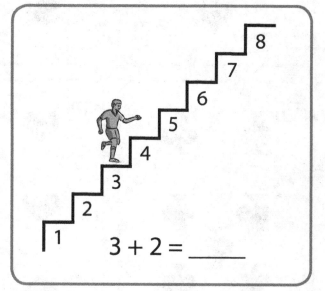

$3 + 2 =$ _____

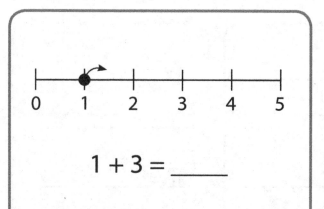

$1 + 3 =$ _____

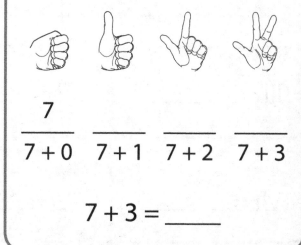

7

_____   _____   _____   _____
$7 + 0$ $7 + 1$ $7 + 2$ $7 + 3$

$7 + 3 =$ _____

     Games, Activities, and Puzzles

Roman Numbers

Look at the Roman playing cards.
Translate the numbers from Roman to English.

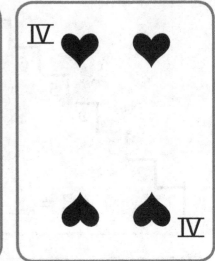

III = _____

V = _____

IV = _____

VII = _____

VI = _____

II = _____

Words and Puzzles

How many more squares than letters?

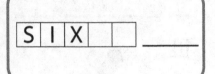 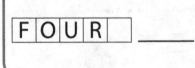 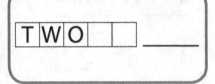

How many more letters than squares?

E L E V EN _____

E I G H TEEN _____

Write the word that fits.

two   seven

five   eight

ten   eleven   thirteen

fifteen   eighteen   twenty

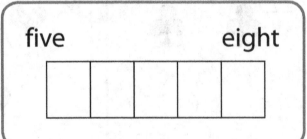

Words and Puzzles *(continued)*

Solve the puzzles with words from the list below.

zero	one	two	three	four	five

	Words with 4 letters	Words with 3 letters
	zer**o**	**o**ne
	fou**r**	**t**wo
	fiv**e**	

The 4-letter word ends with _____ , _____ or _____ .

The 3-letter word starts with _____ or _____ .

Which letter is in both lists? _____ .

Solve the puzzle.

Solve the puzzle.

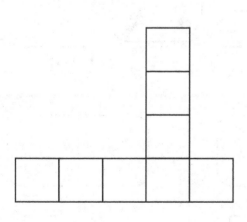

	Words with 4 letters	Words with 3 letters
	zer**o**	thr**e**e
	fou**r**	
	fiv**e**	

Five-Dot Dominoes

page xxx

All of these dominoes have a total of 5 dots.

☐ Draw the missing dots on the blank side.

☐ Finish the number sentence.

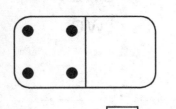 4 + ☐ = 5

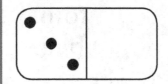 3 + ☐ = 5

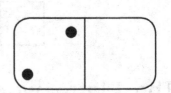 2 + ☐ = 5

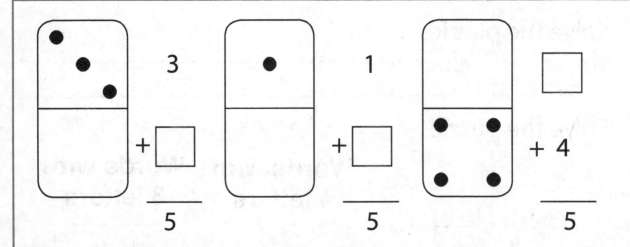

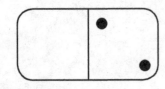 5 = ☐ + 2

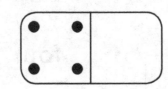 5 = 4 + ☐

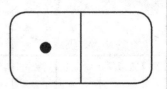 5 = 1 + ☐

Food Sale

14¢

9¢

11¢

12¢

15¢

10¢

12¢

13¢

No unauthorized copying

Games, Activities, and Puzzles

Food Sale (continued)

Mona's Market

Item: _____

Price: _____

Money Given: _____

Change Received: _____

Mona's Market

Item: _____

Price: _____

Money Given: _____

Change Received: _____

Mona's Market

Item: _____

Price: _____

Money Given: _____

Change Received: _____

Mona's Market

Item: _____

Price: _____

Money Given: _____

Change Received: _____

Mona's Market

Item: _____

Price: _____

Money Given: _____

Change Received: _____

Mona's Market

Item: _____

Price: _____

Money Given: _____

Change Received: _____

Mona's Market

Item: _____

Price: _____

Money Given: _____

Change Received: _____

Mona's Market

Item: _____

Price: _____

Money Given: _____

Change Received: _____

Hundreds Charts and Calendars

Hundreds Chart

1	2	3	4	5	6	7	8	9	10
11	12	13	14	15	16	17	18	19	20
21	22	23	24	25	26	27	28	29	30

How many numbers are in each row? _____
Directly under a number, you add _____ to it.

Calendar

Su	M	T	W	Th	F	Sa
			1	2	3	4
5	6	7	8	9	10	11
12	13	14	15	16	17	18

How many numbers are in each row? _____
Directly under a number, you add _____ to it.

Modelling Subtraction

Subtract.

a)    5 – 3 = _____

b)   9 – 3 = _____

c)   7 – 4 = _____

d)   9 – 2 = _____

e)   4 – 1 = _____

f)   6 – 4 = _____

g)   5 – 2 = _____

Modelling Subtraction

Models of Counting Back

Subtract.

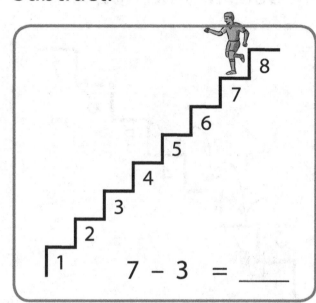

7 – 3 = _____

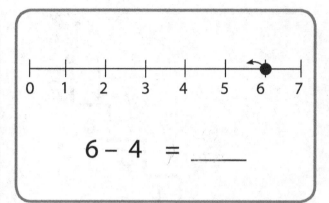

6 – 4 = _____

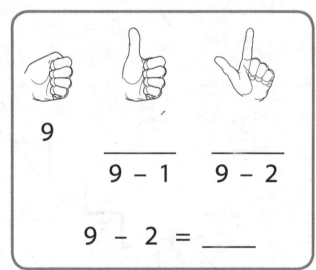

9

_____   _____
9 – 1   9 – 2

9 – 2 = _____

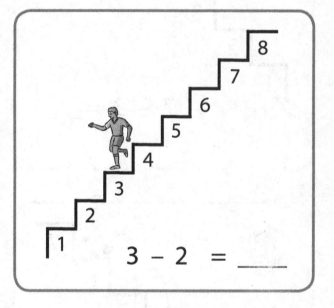

3 – 2 = _____

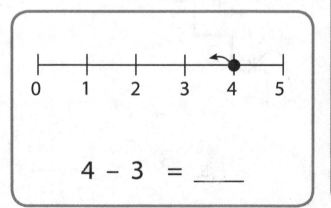

4 – 3 = _____

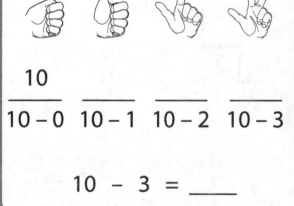

10

_____   _____   _____   _____
10 – 0   10 – 1   10 – 2   10 – 3

10 – 3 = _____

No unauthorized copying   **Games, Activities, and Puzzles**

Subtracting on Stairs

Liam goes down 3 steps. Where does he end up?

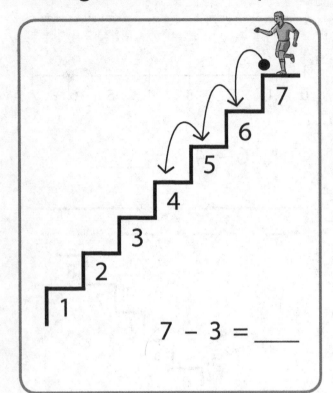

7 – 3 = ____

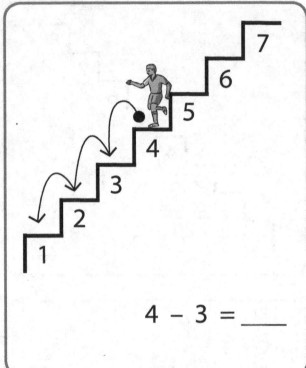

4 – 3 = ____

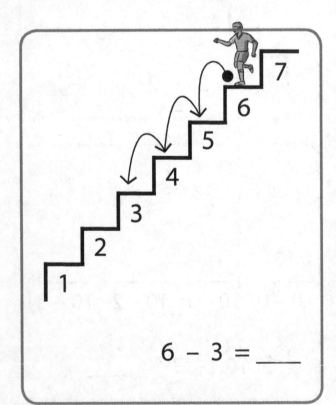

6 – 3 = ____

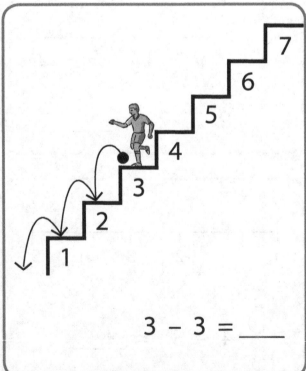

3 – 3 = ____

Subtracting on Stairs *(continued)*

Count the steps.
Fill in the blanks.

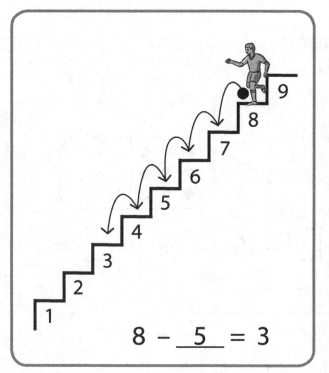

8 – __5__ = 3

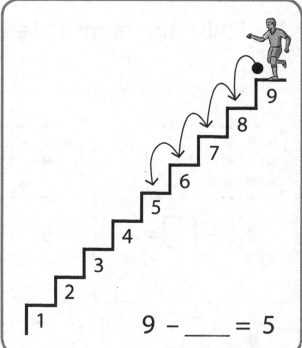

9 – ____ = 5

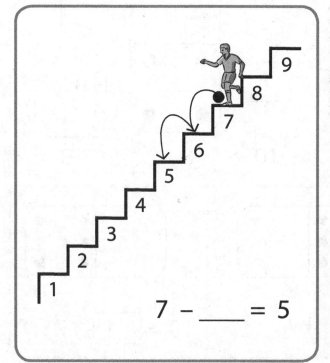

7 – ____ = 5

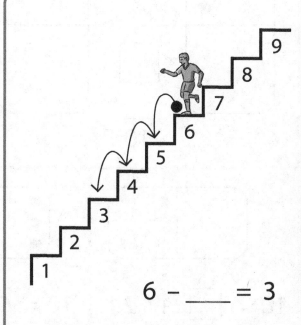

6 – ____ = 3

Ten-Dot Dominoes

All of these dominoes have a total of 10 dots.

☐ Draw the missing dots on the blank side.

☐ Finish the number sentence.

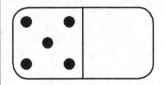

$8 + \boxed{} = 10$

$5 + \boxed{} = 10$

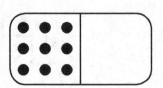

$9 + \boxed{} = 10$

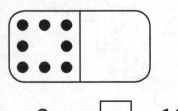

3

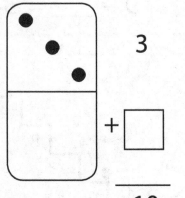

$+ \boxed{}$

$\overline{10}$

1

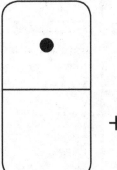

$+ \boxed{}$

$\overline{10}$

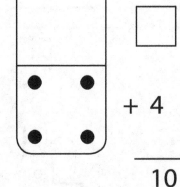

$\boxed{}$

$+ 4$

$\overline{10}$

$10 = \boxed{} + 2$

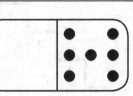

$10 = 6 + \boxed{}$

$10 = \boxed{} + 7$

The Twenties

Fill in the blanks.

twenty			=	20
twenty	–	one	=	21
twenty	–	_____	=	22
_____	–	three	=	23
_____	–	four	=	24
twenty	–	five	=	_____
twenty	–	_____	=	26
_____	–	seven	=	27
_____	–	_____	=	28
twenty	–	_____	=	9

The numbers above are the 20s (twenties).
Write down the 30s (thirties).

Word Stories

Look at the number sentences and create your own word problems that match.

3 + 1 = 4	
7 = 5 + 2	
6 + 3 = 9	
8 = 4 + 4	

Word Stories (continued)

5 = 8 – 3	
4 – 3 = 1	
7 = 9 – 2	
10 – 10 = 0	

No unauthorized copying

Games, Activities, and Puzzles

Word Stories *(continued)*

2 + 7 = 9	
7 = 10 − 3	
10 = 4 + 6	
4 − 2 = 2	

Connect the Dots by 2s

Start at 2 and skip count by 2s to 80 to create a picture.

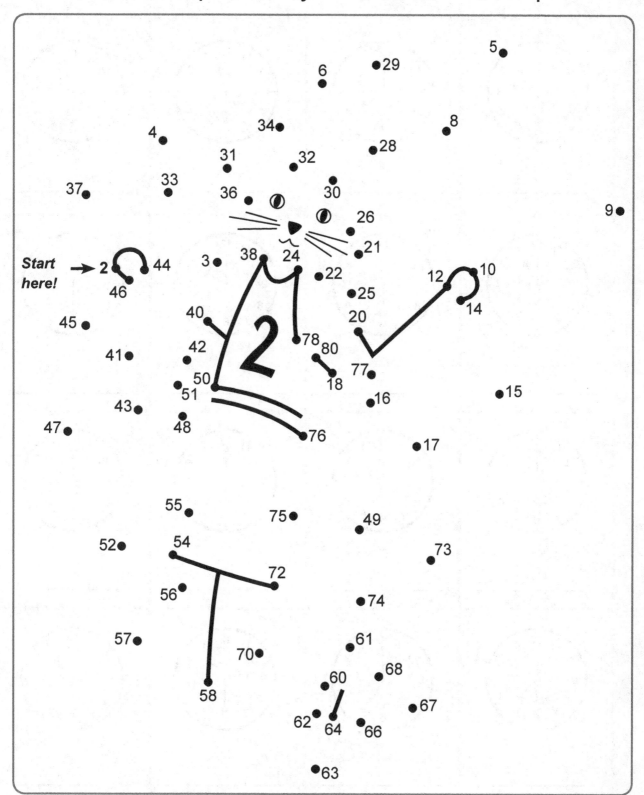

Extra Practice: Time

Write the time for each clock.

Matching Analogue to Digital

Matching Analogue to Digital (continued)

TV Guide

My TV Guide

Name of Show	Start Time	Finish Time	How long?
Day: _____	: _____	: _____	
Day: _____	: _____	: _____	
Day: _____	: _____	: _____	
Day: _____	: _____	: _____	

No unauthorized copying

UNIT 1

Number Sense 1

NS1-1 Counting

☐ Colour.

3 ants

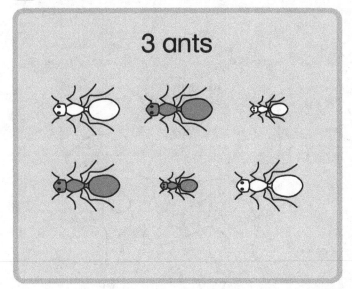

3 spiders

3 bubbles

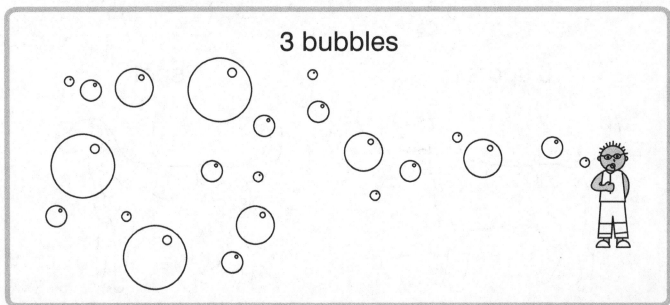

NS1-1 **Counting** (continued)

☐ Colour.

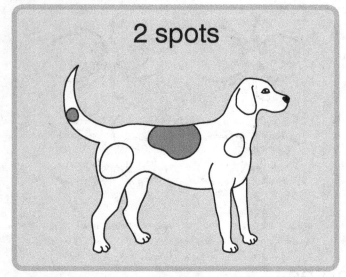

2 spots

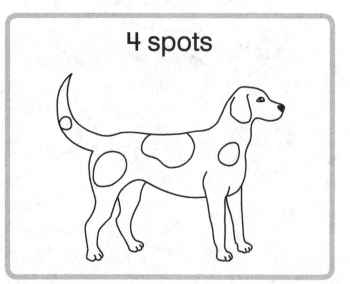

4 spots

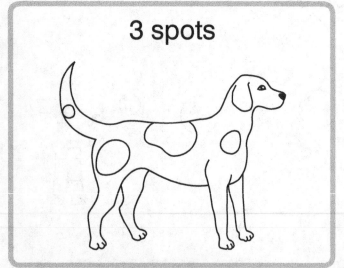

3 spots

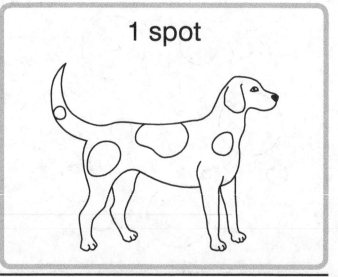

1 spot

NS1-2 Match by Counting

☐ Match by number.

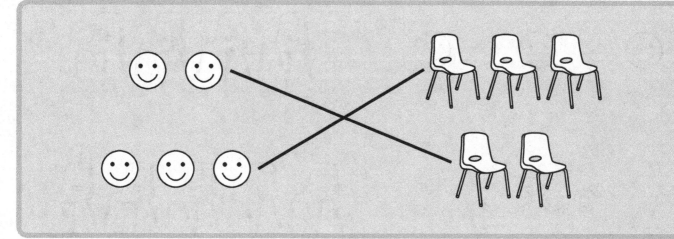

NS1-2 **Match by Counting** (continued)

☐ Match by number.

NS1-2 **Match by Counting** (continued)

☐ Match by number.

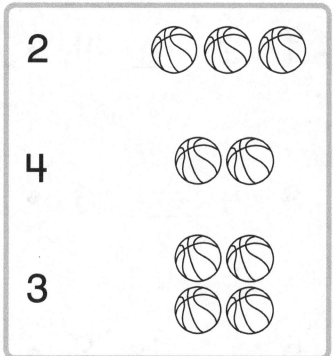

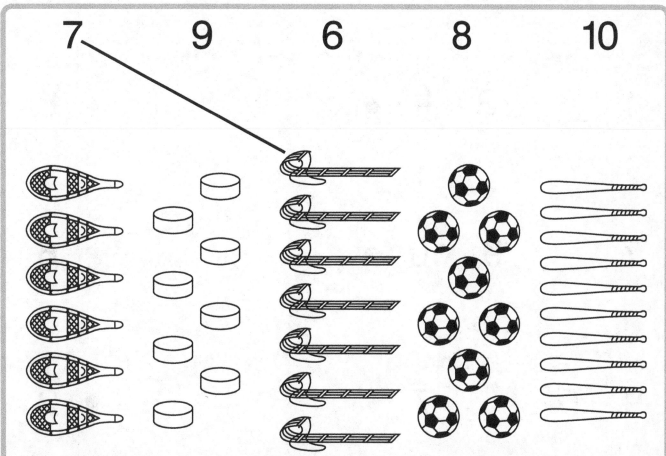

NS1-3 **There Is Order Here**

☐ Find the missing number.

1 2 ___ 4 •   • 7

3 4 ___ 6 •   3

6 ___ 8 9 •   • 5

1 ___ 3 4 •   • 8

7 ___ 9 10 •   • 6

4 5 ___ 7 •   • 2

NS1-3 There Is Order Here (continued)

☐ Join the dots in order.

| 1 | 2 | 3 | 4 | 5 | 6 | 7 | 8 | 9 |

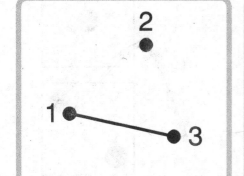

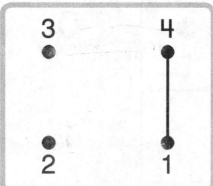

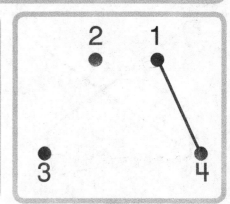

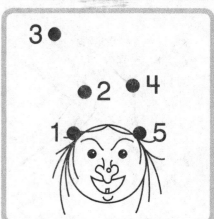

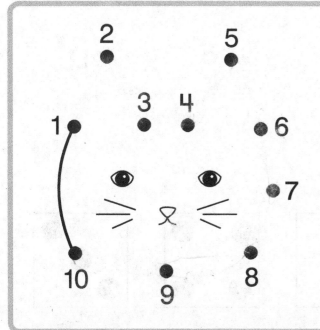

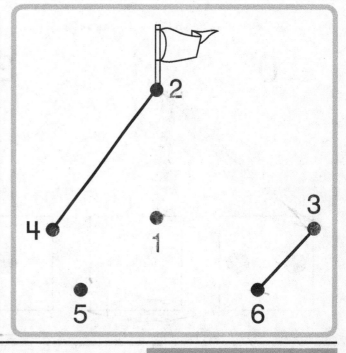

NS1-4 The Number that Means Nothing

☐ Match by number.

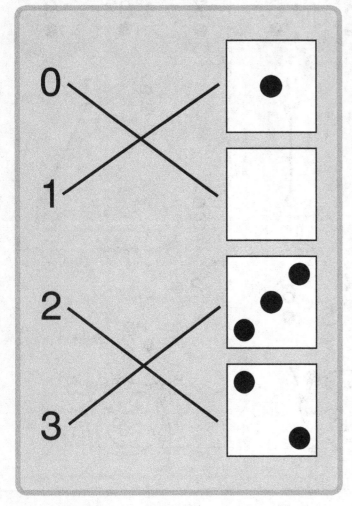

0	1	2	3	4

NS1-4 The Number that Means Nothing (continued)

☐ Match by number.

3	⬤ ⬤
1	⬤ ⬤ ⬤
0	⬤
2	

2	⬤⬤⬤
3	
1	⬤
0	⬤ ⬤

3   1   4   0   2

 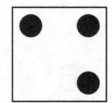  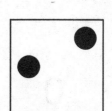 

NS1-4 The Number that Means Nothing (continued)

0	1	2	3	4	5	6	7	8	9

☐ Circle the numbers.

③ 3	Ʇ 4	5 5
6 6	8 8	3 3
9 9	9 9	2 2

7 7 7 7	7 9 8 4

Bonus

7 3 0 8 9 5 2 0

NS1-5 Writing Numbers

Join the dots in order.

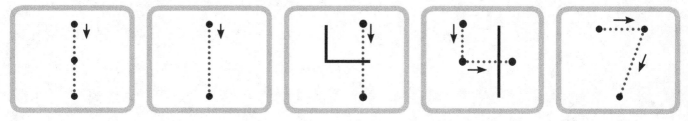

Trace.

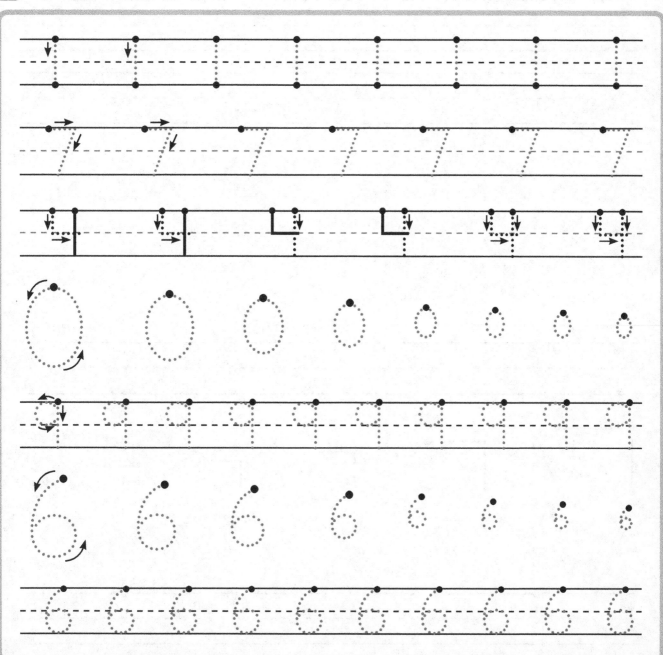

No unauthorized copying

NS1-5 Writing Numbers (continued)

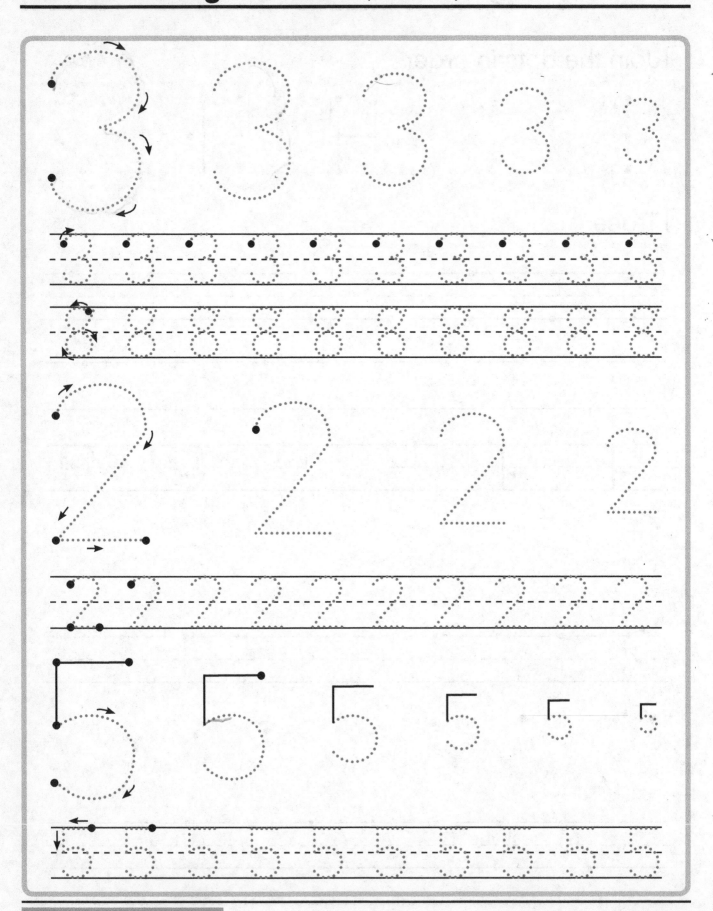

NS1-5 Writing Numbers (continued)

How many legs?

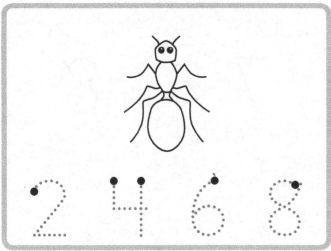

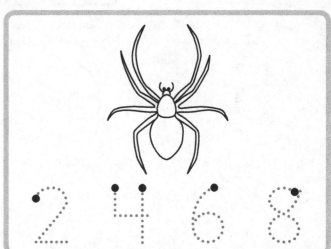

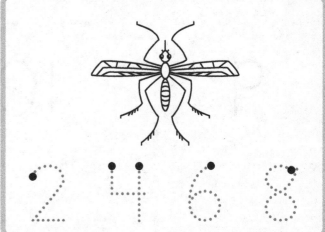

Bonus: Insects have 6 legs. Circle the insects.

NS1-5 **Writing Numbers** (continued)

☐ Press the number on a .
☐ Draw what you see.

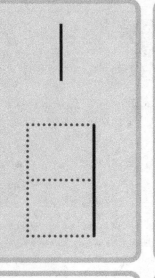

1

2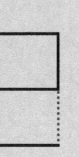

3

4

5

6

7

8

9

10

Bonus

4 3 2

NS1-6 Counting Using a Chart

How many ants?

1 2 3 4 5 6 7 8 9 10

There are ___6___ ants.

1 2 3 4 5 6 7 8 9 10

There are _____ ants.

1 2 3 4 5 6 7 8 9 10

There are _____ ants.

1 2 3 4 5 6 7 8 9 10

There are _____ ants.

JUMP AT HOME GRADE 1   No unauthorized copying   **Number Sense 1**

NS1-6 **Counting Using a Chart** *(continued)*

How many blocks?

There are __**7**__ blocks.

There are _____ blocks.

There are _____ blocks.

There are _____ blocks.

NS1-7 More and Less

The monkey wants **more** bananas.

☐ Count the bananas.
☐ Circle the group with more.

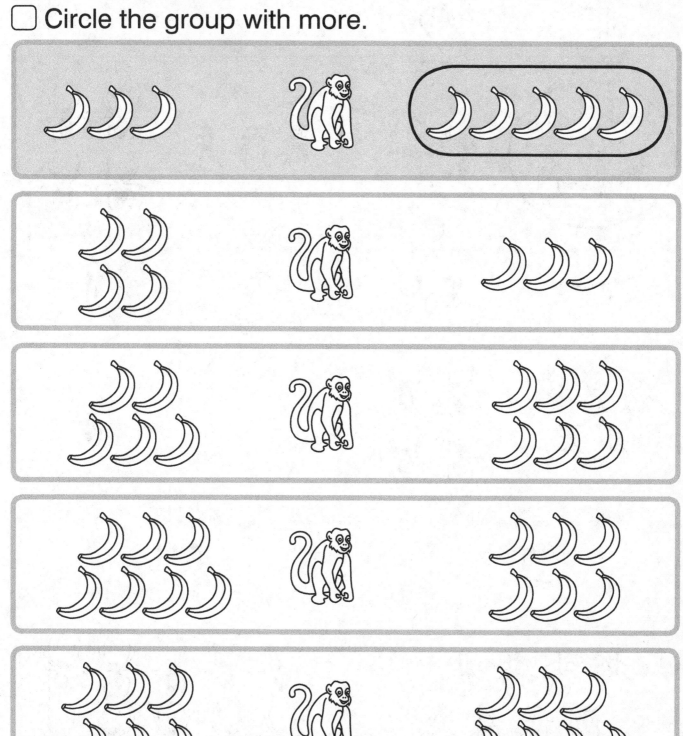

NS1-7 **More and Less** (continued)

☐ Trace the numbers.
☐ Circle the group with **more**.

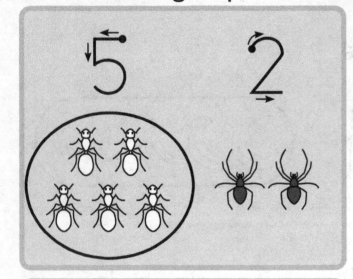

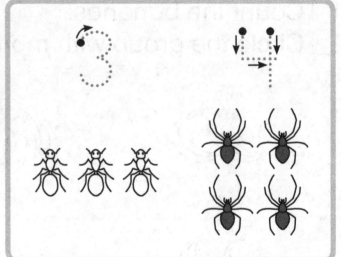

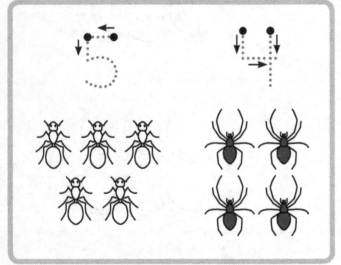

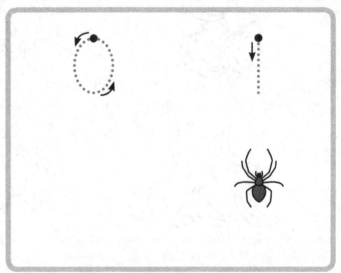

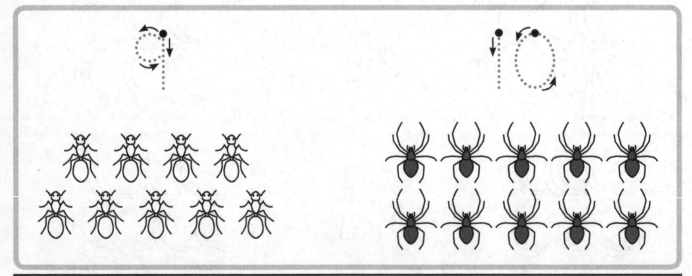

NS1-7 **More and Less** (continued)

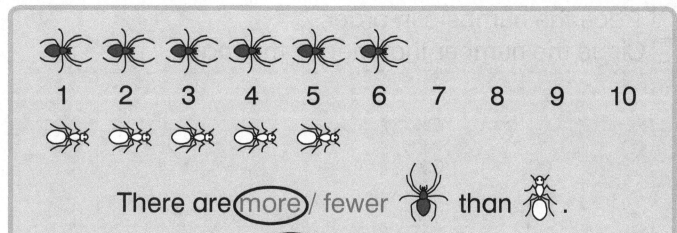

There are (more) / fewer 🕷 than 🐜 .

6 is (more) / less than 5.

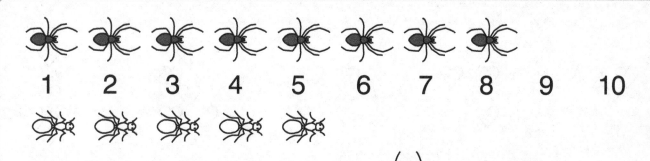

There are more / fewer 🕷 than 🐜 .

4 is more / less than 6.

There are more / fewer 🕷 than 🐜 .

8 is more / less than 5.

NS1-7 **More and Less** (continued)

☐ Trace the numbers in order.
☐ Circle the number that means the **most**.

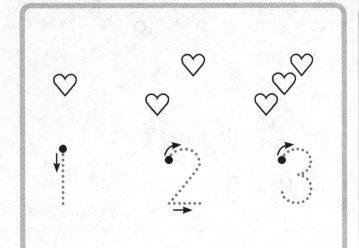
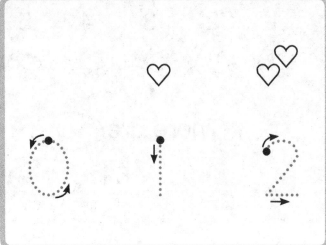

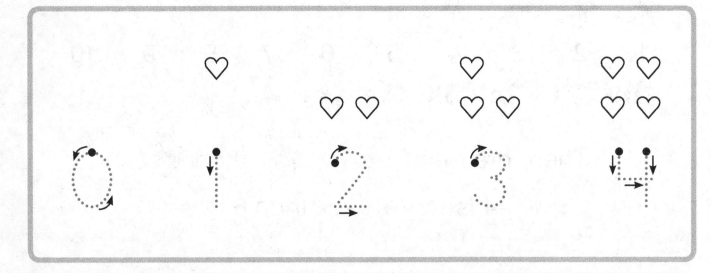

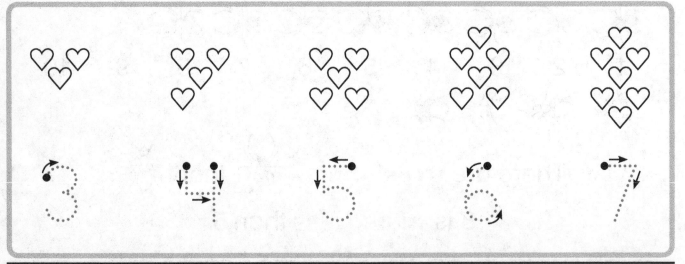

NS1-7 **More and Less** (continued)

☐ Trace the number that means **more**.
☐ Circle the number that means **less**.

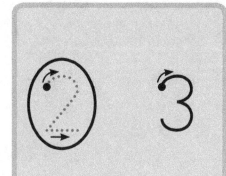
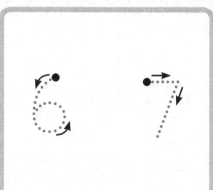
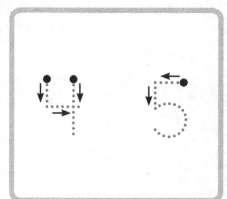
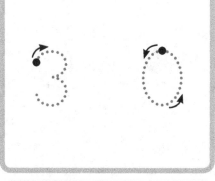

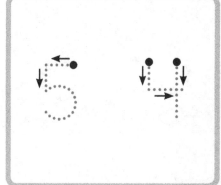
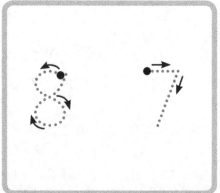
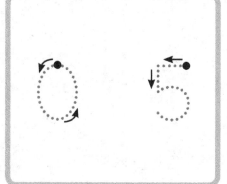
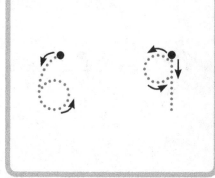
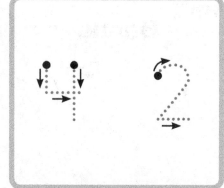
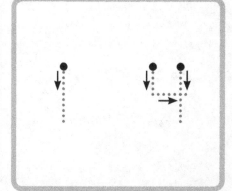

NS1-7 **More and Less** (continued)

☐ Trace the number that means the **most**.
☐ Circle the number that means the **least**.

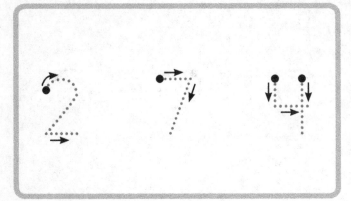

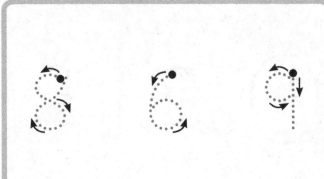

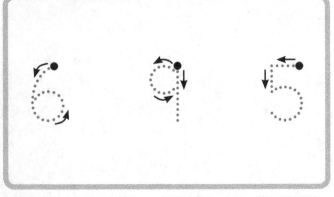

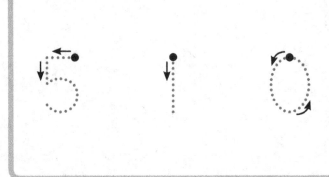

Bonus

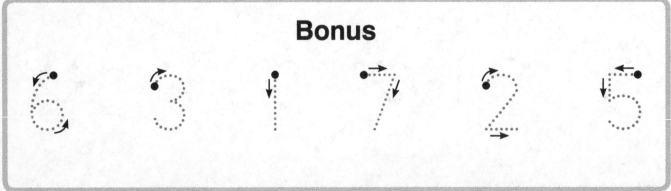

NS1-8 One-to-One Correspondence

◻ Pair the ◻ and △.

Are there more ◻ or △?

There are more ___◻___.

There are more _____.

There are more _____.

There are more _____.

NS1-8 One-to-One Correspondence *(continued)*

Can each mouse have a piece of cheese?

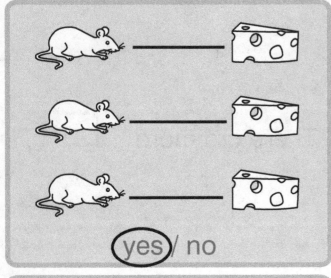

yes / no

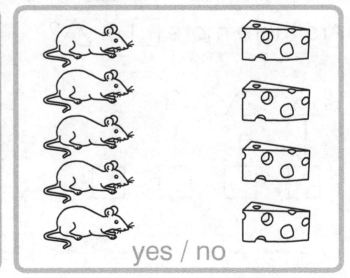

yes / no

yes / no

yes / no

yes / no

NS1-9 How Many More?

How many more ◯ than △?

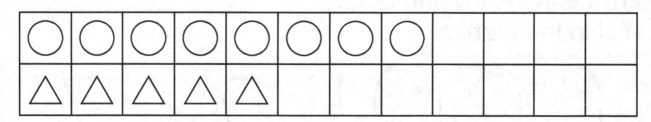

There are _____ more ◯ than △.

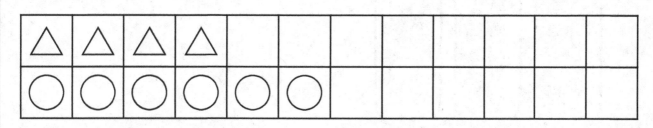

There are _____ more ◯ than △.

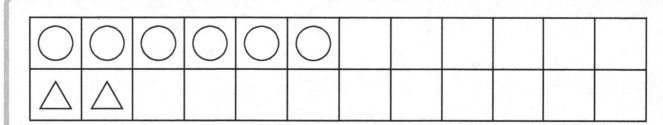

There are _____ more ◯ than △.

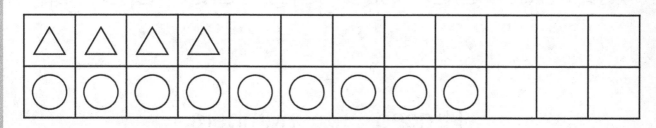

There are _____ more ◯ than △.

NS1-10 Counting On

☐ Circle the matching numbers.
☐ Trace the extra numbers.
☐ Fill in the blanks.

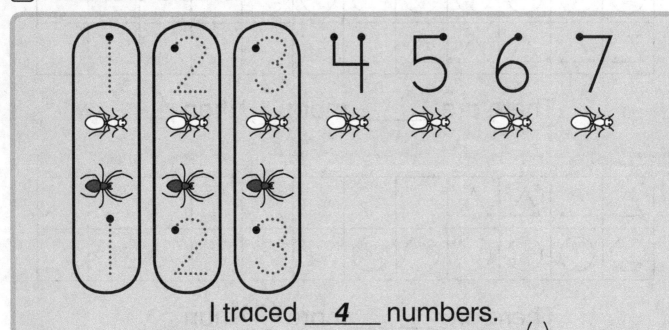

I traced ___4___ numbers.

There are ___4___ more 🐜 than 🕷.

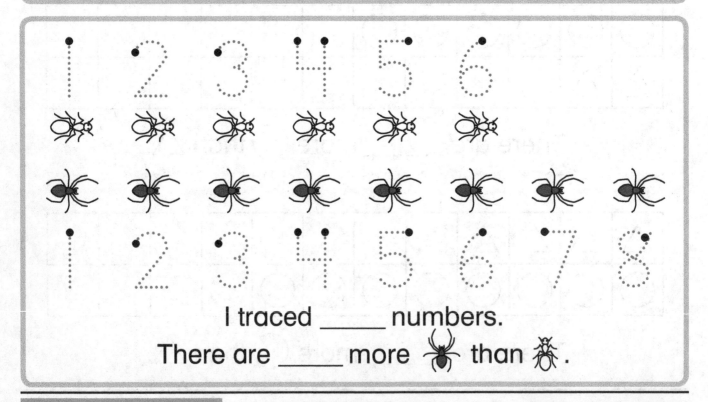

I traced _____ numbers.

There are _____ more 🕷 than 🐜.

NS1-10 **Counting On** *(continued)*

- ☐ Match the 🐜 and 🕷.
- ☐ Trace the extra numbers.
- ☐ Fill in the blanks.

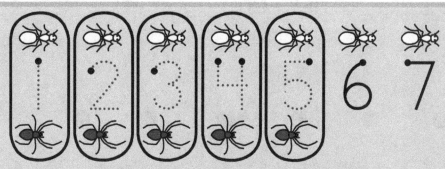

I traced ___**2**___ numbers.

There are ___**2**___ more 🐜 than 🕷.

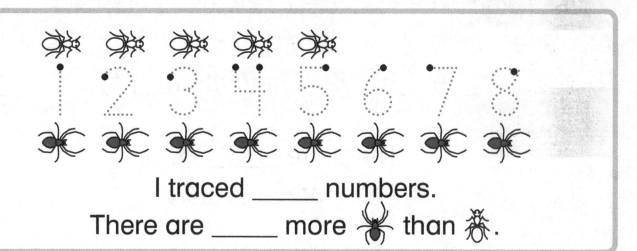

I traced _____ numbers.

There are _____ more 🕷 than 🐜.

I traced _____ numbers.

NS1-10 Counting On (continued)

☐ Trace the extra numbers.
☐ Fill in the blanks.

There are ___7___ ●.

● ● ● ● ● ● ●

1 2 3 4 5 6 7 8 9

○ ○ ○ ○ ○ ○ ○ ○ ○

___9___ is ___2___ more than ___7___.

There are _____ ●.
There are _____ ○.

● ● ● ● ● ● ● ●

1 2 3 4 5 6 7 8

○ ○ ○

_____ is _____ more than _____.

NS1-10 **Counting On** (continued)

☐ Trace the dotted numbers.

How many numbers did you trace?

0 1 2 3 4 5 6 7

7 is __3__ more than 4.

0 1 2 3 4 5

5 is _____ more than 1.

0 1 2 3 4 5

5 is _____ more than 3.

0 1 2 3 4 5 6

6 is _____ more than 5.

No unauthorized copying

NS1-10 **Counting On** (continued)

☐ Trace the dotted numbers.
☐ Fill in the blanks.

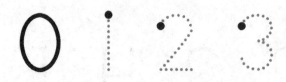

3 is _____ more than 0.

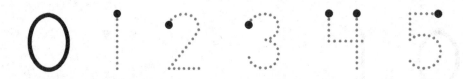

5 is _____ more than 0.

4 is _____ more than 0.

2 is _____ more than 0.

6 is _____ more than 0.

8 is _____ more than 0.

9 is _____ more than 0.

Number Sense 1 · No unauthorized copying · **JUMP AT HOME GRADE 1**

NS1-10 Counting On *(continued)*

1	2	3	4	5	6	7	8	9

4	5	6
4 is 0 more than 4.	5 is 1 more than 4.	6 is 2 more than 4.

9 is _____ more than 6.

8 is _____ more than 3.

9 is _____ more than 7.

6 is _____ more than 3.

7 is _____ more than 5.

3 is _____ more than 1.

5 is _____ more than 0.

4 is _____ more than 1.

NS1-11 Counting to 20

1	2	3	4	5	6	7	8	9	10
11	12	13	14	15	16	17	18	19	20

How many...

stars?

_14_

leaves?

_____

teeth?

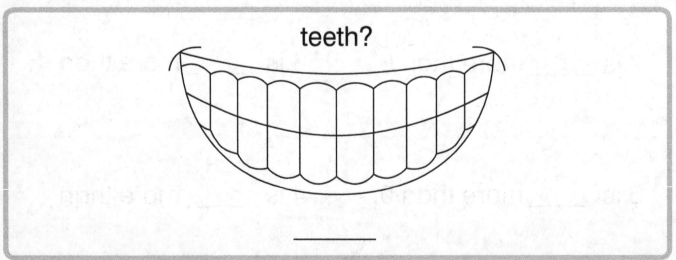

_____

NS1-12 Using a Chart to Count to 20

What comes next?

1	2	3	4	5	6	7	8	9	10
11	12	13	14	15	16	17	18	19	20

3 ____   10 ____   17 ____

1	2	3	4	5	6	7	8	9	10
11	12	13	14	15	16	17	18	19	20

5 ____   9 ____   13 ____

1	2	3	4	5	6	7	8	9	10
11	12	13	14	15	16	17	18	19	20

16 ____   2 ____   11 ____

NS1-12 **Using a Chart to Count to 20** *(continued)*

What comes next?

1	2	3	4	5	6	7	8	9	10
11	12	13	14	15	16	17	18	19	20

6 ___

8 ___

17 ___

4 ___

10 ___

19 ___

18 ___

11 ___

9 ___

Bonus: Cover the chart.

3 ___

12 ___

16 ___

NS1-13 Tens and Ones Blocks

☐ Count the tens blocks and ones blocks on the chart.

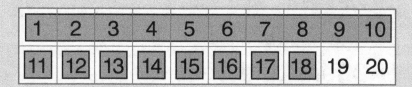

18 is __1__ tens block and __8__ ones blocks.

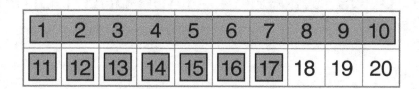

15 is _____ tens block and _____ ones blocks.

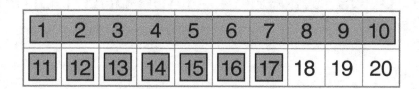

17 is _____ tens block and _____ ones blocks.

11 is _____ tens block and _____ ones block.

NS1-13 Tens and Ones Blocks *(continued)*

Hundreds chart:

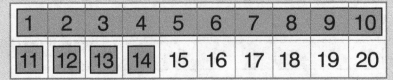

Tens and ones blocks:

14 is 1 ten and 4 ones.

What number does each set represent?

1 ten and 6 ones is __*16*__.

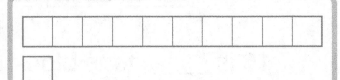

1 ten and 1 one is ____.

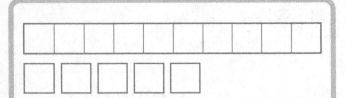

1 ten and 5 ones is ____.

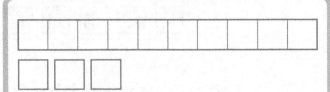

1 ten and 3 ones is ____.

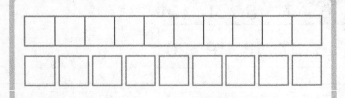

1 ten and 9 ones is ____.

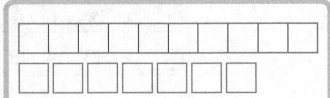

1 ten and 7 ones is ____.

NS1-14 Ordering Numbers

☐ Write the ▨ numbers from smallest to largest.

1	2	3	4	5	6	7	8	9	10

_____ _____ _____

1	2	3	4
5	6	7	8
9	10	11	12

_____ _____ _____

9	10	11	12
13	14	15	16
17	18	19	20

_____ _____ _____

1	2	3	4	5
6	7	8	9	10
11	12	13	14	15
16	17	18	19	20

_____ _____ _____

1	2	3	4	5
6	7	8	9	10
11	12	13	14	15
16	17	18	19	20

_____ _____ _____

1	2	3	4	5	6	7	8	9	10
11	12	13	14	15	16	17	18	19	20

_____ _____ _____ _____ _____

NS1-14 Ordering Numbers (continued)

☐ Shade the given numbers.
☐ Order them from smallest to largest.

5   8   2

1	2	3	4	5
6	7	8	9	10

2 ___ 5 ___ 8 ___

10   6   1

1	2	3	4	5
6	7	8	9	10

___ ___ ___

16   13   14

11	12	13	14	15
16	17	18	19	20

___ ___ ___

11   20   17

11	12	13	14	15
16	17	18	19	20

___ ___ ___

14   6   3   19   10

1	2	3	4	5	6	7	8	9	10
11	12	13	14	15	16	17	18	19	20

___ ___ ___ ___ ___

2   17   4   8   16

1	2	3	4	5	6	7	8	9	10
11	12	13	14	15	16	17	18	19	20

___ ___ ___ ___ ___

NS1-15 Comparing to 5 or 10

☐ Count the fingers up.

How many more than 5?

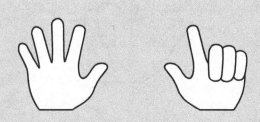

__7__ is __2__ more than 5.

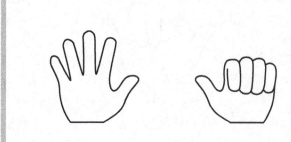

____ is ____ more than 5.

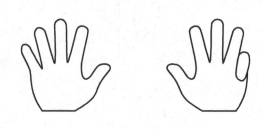

____ is ____ more than 5.

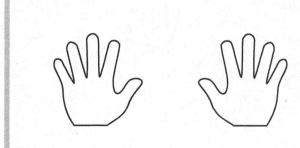

____ is ____ more than 5.

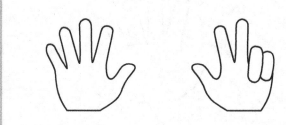

____ is ____ more than 5.

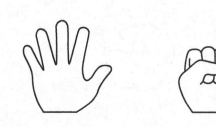

____ is ____ more than 5.

NS1-15 Comparing to 5 or 10 *(continued)*

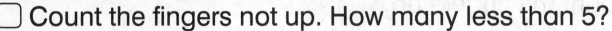

- ☐ Count the fingers up.
- ☐ Count the fingers not up. How many less than 5?

__1__ is __4__ less than 5.

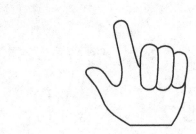

____ is ____ less than 5.

____ is ____ less than 5.

____ is ____ less than 5.

____ is ____ less than 5.

____ is ____ less than 5.

NS1-15 **Comparing to 5 or 10** (continued)

How many more than 10?

1	2	3	4	5	6	7	8	9	10
11	12	13	14	15	16	17	18	19	20

14 is __4__ more than 10.

17 is ____ more than 10.

19 is ____ more than 10.

15 is ____ more than 10.

11 is ____ more than 10.

18 is ____ more than 10.

16 is ____ more than 10.

12 is ____ more than 10.

NS1-16 Adding

How many in total?

3 flags + 2 flags = _____ flags in total

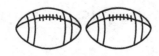

3 balls + 2 balls = _____ balls in total

$$3 + 2 = \underline{\quad}$$

_____ trees in total = 2 trees + 4 trees

_____ children = 2 girls + 4 boys

$$\underline{\quad} = 2 + 4$$

NS1-16 Adding *(continued)*

☐ Add.

4   +   3   =   _____

3   +   5   =   _____

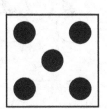

5   +   2   =   _____

2   +   6   =   _____

NS1-16 Adding *(continued)*

☐ Add 0.

___ **3** ___   +   ___ **0** ___   =   ___ **3** ___

___   +   ___   =   ___

___   =   ___   +   ___

___   =   ___   +   ___

Bonus

0 + 17 = ____   ____ = 14 + 0

NS1-17 More Adding

☐ Add.

☆ ☆   2
☆   + 1

☆ ☆   2
☆ ☆ ☆ + 3

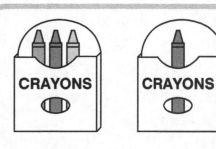
  1
  3
  2
+ 3

☆ ☆   2
☆ ☆ + 2

☆   1
☆ ☆ ☆ ☆ + 4

How many crayons altogether?

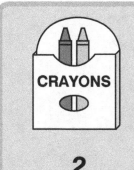   2

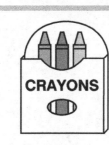   ___

3 + 1 = ___

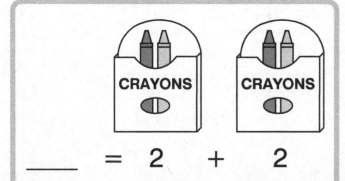   ___ = 2 + 2

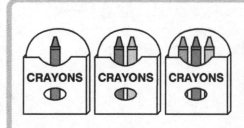   1 + 2 + 3 = ___

NS1-17 More Adding *(continued)*

☐ Draw a picture to add.

3 + 2 + 6 = ____

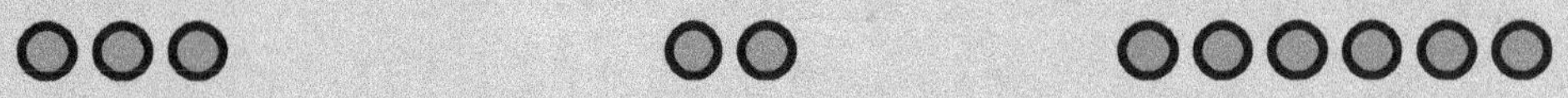

○○○   ○○   ○○○○○○

4 + 2 + 3 = ____

3
2
+ 5
☐

4
2
+ 7
☐

NS1-17 **More Adding** (continued)

There are 10 apples in the basket.

How many apples are there altogether?

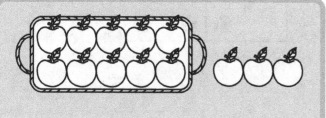

10 + __3__ = __13__

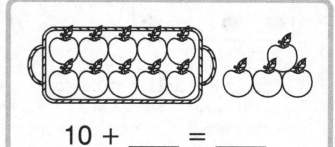

10 + ___ = ___

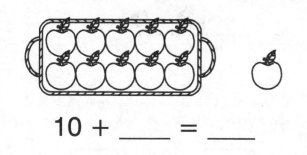

10 + ___ = ___

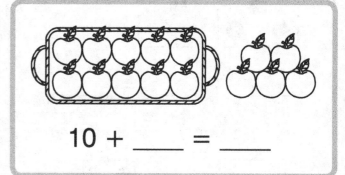

10 + ___ = ___

☐ Add.

10 + 2 = ___	10 + 7 = ___
10 + 6 = ___	10 + 8 = ___

10 + 5	10 + 3	10 + 4	10 + 1	10 + 9

NS1-18 Addition and Order

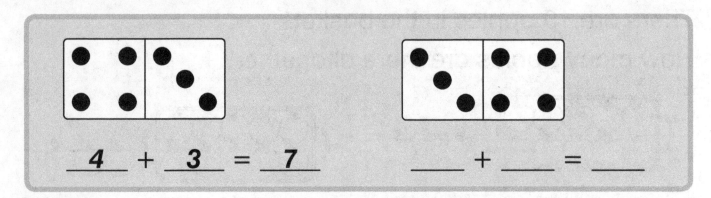

___4___ + ___3___ = ___7___   _____ + _____ = _____

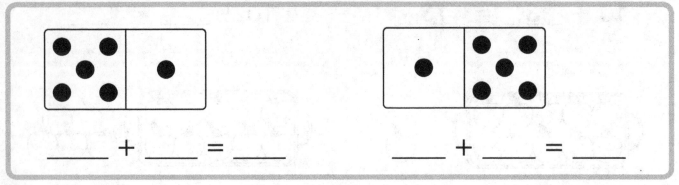

_____ + _____ = _____   _____ + _____ = _____

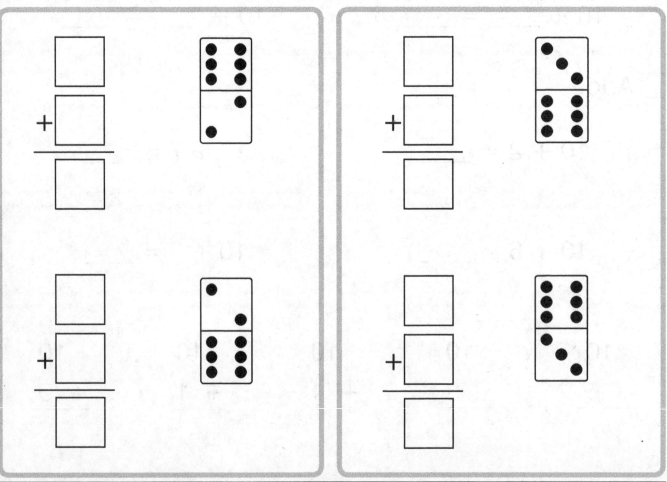

NS1-18 Addition and Order (continued)

☐ Write one addition sentence for both pictures.

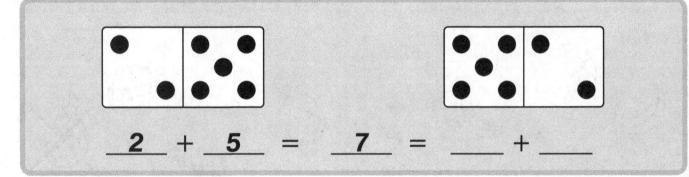

__2__ + __5__ = __7__ = ____ + ____

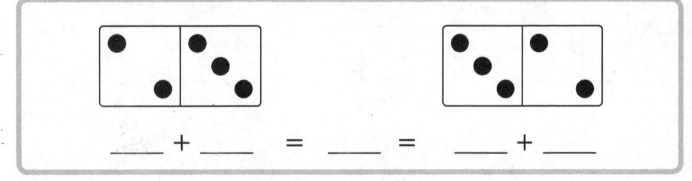

____ + ____ = ____ = ____ + ____

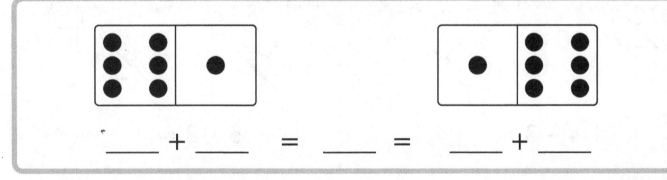

____ + ____ = ____ = ____ + ____

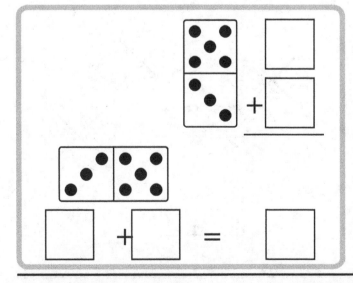

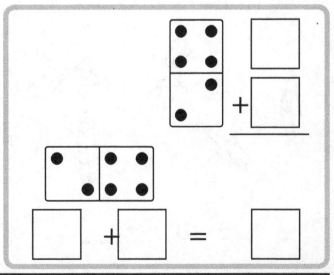

NS1-19 Subtracting

☐ Take away.

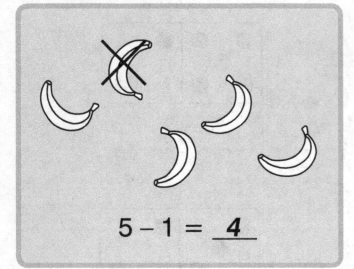

$5 - 1 = \underline{\ 4\ }$

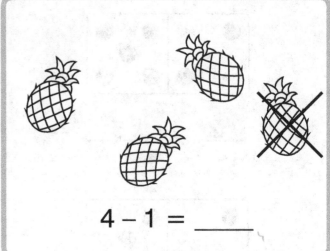

$4 - 1 = \underline{\hspace{2cm}}$

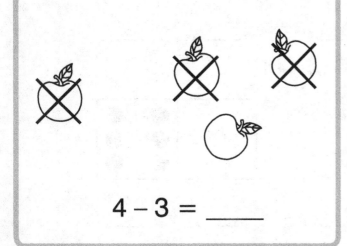

$4 - 3 = \underline{\hspace{2cm}}$

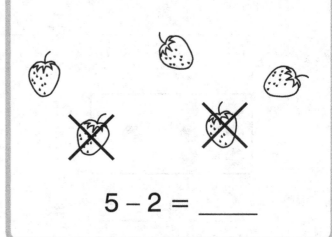

$5 - 2 = \underline{\hspace{2cm}}$

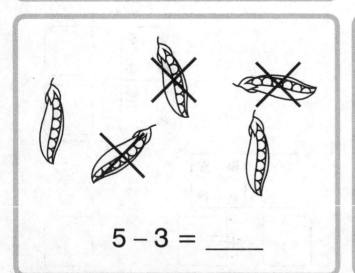

$5 - 3 = \underline{\hspace{2cm}}$

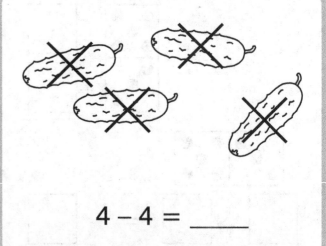

$4 - 4 = \underline{\hspace{2cm}}$

NS1-19 Subtracting *(continued)*

☐ Cross out the correct number.
☐ Subtract.

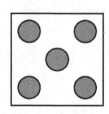

4 − 1 = __*3*__

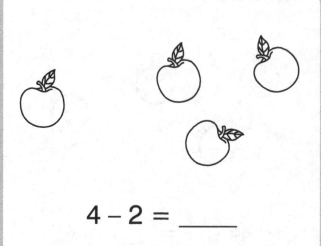

4 − 2 = _____

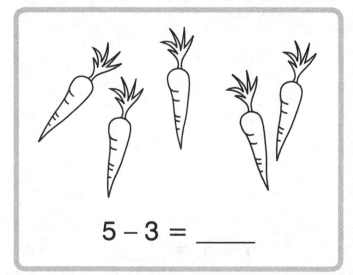

5 − 3 = _____

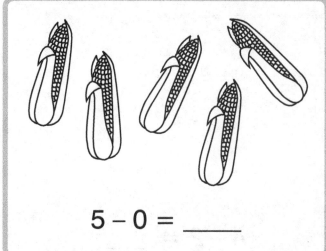

5 − 0 = _____

5 − 2 = _____

4 − 3 = _____

3 − 1 = _____

NS1-19 Subtracting *(continued)*

☐ Draw the first number of circles.
☐ Cross out the second number of circles.
☐ Subtract.

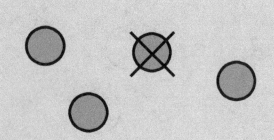

$4 - 1 = \underline{\ \textbf{3}\ }$

$5 - 3 = \underline{\hspace{1.5cm}}$

$4 - 2 = \underline{\hspace{1.5cm}}$

$6 - 5 = \underline{\hspace{1.5cm}}$

$3 - 3 = \underline{\hspace{1.5cm}}$

$4 - 0 = \underline{\hspace{1.5cm}}$

NS1-19 **Subtracting** (continued)

Eric has 10 apples.
Dillon takes away 4 apples.
How many are left?

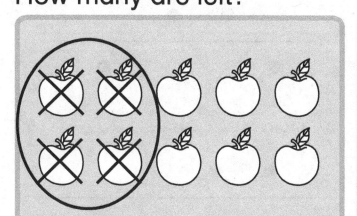

10 − 4 = **6**

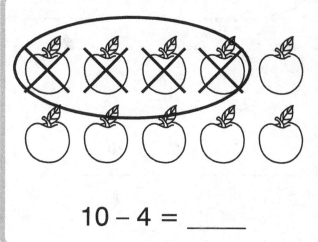

10 − 4 = _____

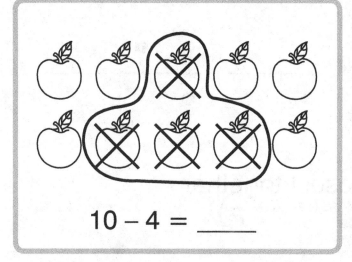

10 − 4 = _____

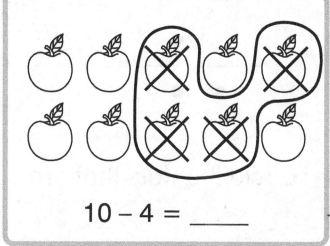

10 − 4 = _____

☐ Take away any 4 apples.

How many are left?

10 − 4 = _____

NS1-20 Closer and Farther

☐ Circle the dots that are closer together.

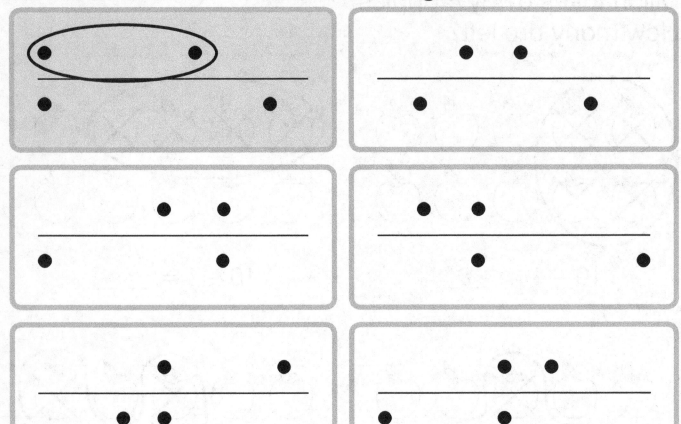

☐ Circle the dots that are closest together.

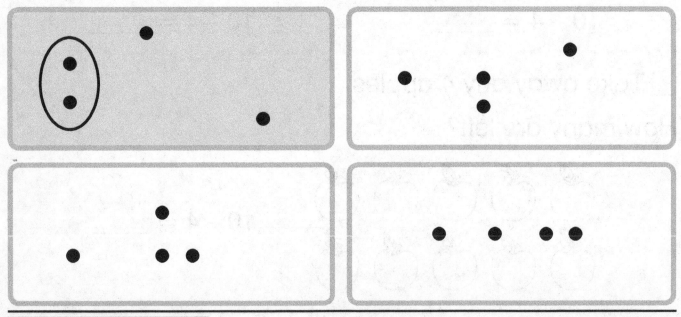

No unauthorized copying

NS1-20 Closer and Farther *(continued)*

☐ Circle the number that 5 is closer to.

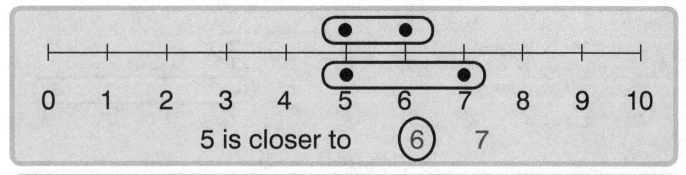

5 is closer to   ⑥   7

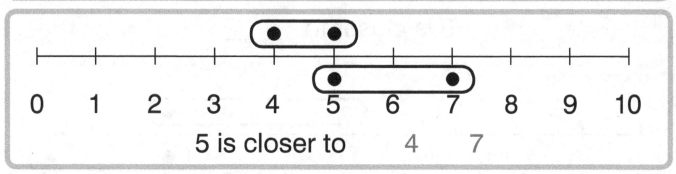

5 is closer to   2   4

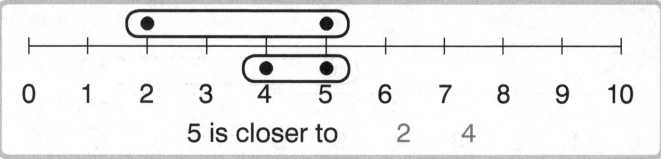

5 is closer to   4   7

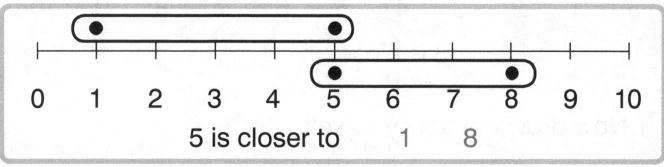

5 is closer to   1   8

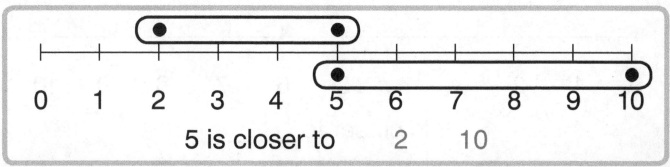

5 is closer to   2   10

NS1-20 **Closer and Farther** (continued)

Is it closer to 5 or 10?

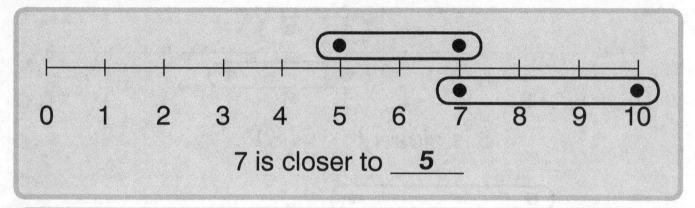

7 is closer to ___5___

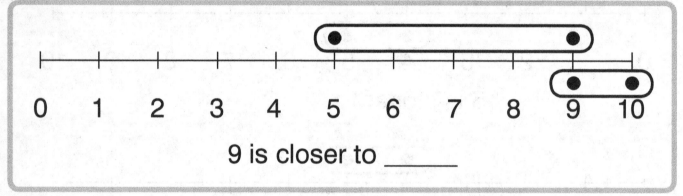

9 is closer to _____

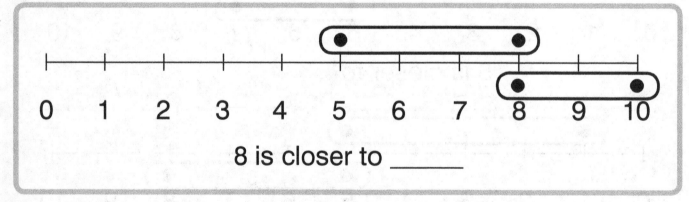

8 is closer to _____

☐ Now draw the dots yourself.

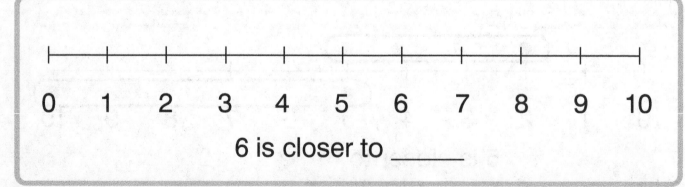

6 is closer to _____

NS1-21 First, Last, and In Between

Circle the first 2 butterflies.

Colour the 2nd butterfly.

Circle the first 5 monkeys.

Colour the 5th monkey.

Circle the first 4 squares.

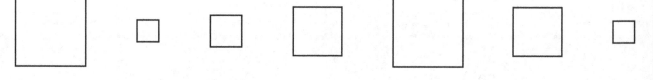

Colour the 4th square.

Circle the first 3 pencils.

 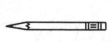 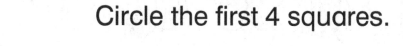    

Colour the 3rd pencil.

NS1-21 First, Last, and In Between (continued)

☐ Circle the first 3 monkeys .
☐ Colour the 3rd monkey.

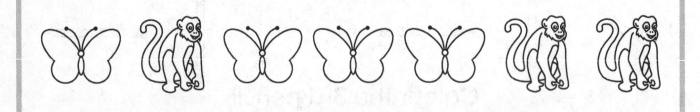

NS1-22 Problems and Puzzles

☐ Trace the letters.

1	2	3	4	5	6	7
d	p	a	y	r	k	f

8	9	10	11	12	13	14
l	c	o	t	h	i	n

15	16	17	18	19	20	21
e	u	s	b	m	g	w

☐ Find the words.

9	3	11

18	13	5	1

19	10	14	6	15	4

15	8	15	2	12	3	14	11

UNIT 2

Patterns and Algebra 1

PA1-1 Cores of Patterns

☐ Circle the core.

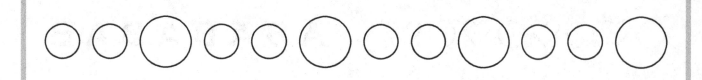

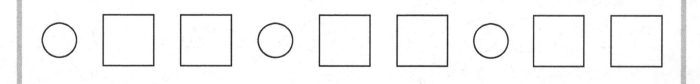

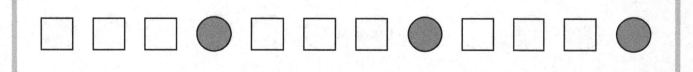

PA1-1 Cores of Patterns (continued)

☐ Circle the core.

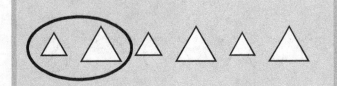

ABABABAB

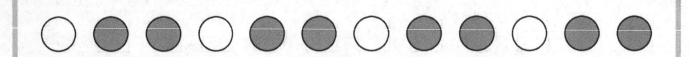

PA1-1 Cores of Patterns (continued)

☐ Circle the core.
☐ How many terms are in the core?

 _3_

 ___

 ___

___

___

___

PA1-1 Cores of Patterns (continued)

☐ Circle the core.
☐ Write the next 3 terms.

(1 2) 1 2 1 2 1 2 1 2   _1_ _2_ _1_

○ △ ○ △ ○ △ ○ △ ○ △ ___ ___ ___

● ✓ ✓ ● ✓ ✓ ● ✓ ✓ ___ ___ ___

○ △ △ ○ △ △ ○ △ △ ___ ___ ___

▫ ▫ ▫ ▫ ▫ ▫ ▫ ▫ ___ ___ ___

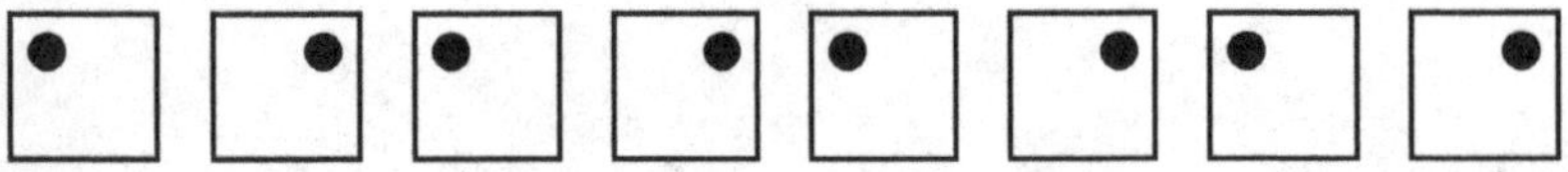

Bonus

A A ∀ A A ∀ A A ∀ ___ ___ ___

PA1-2 A Core that Ends the Way It Starts

The core is circled.

☐ Check the first and last terms in the core.

Are they the same or not?

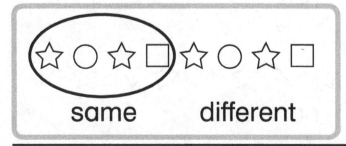
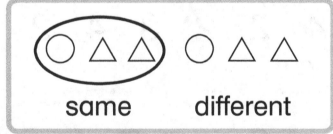
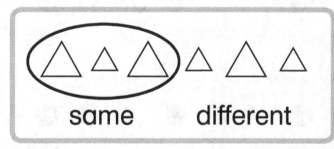
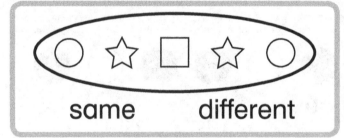
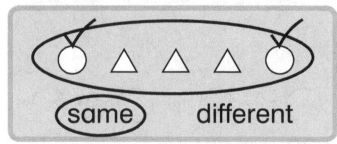
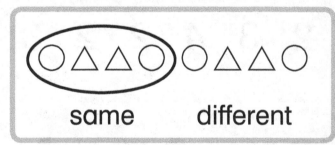
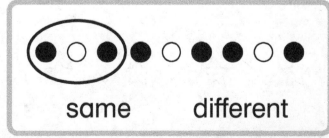
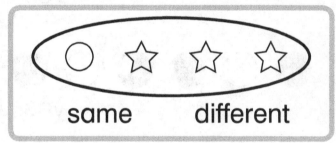
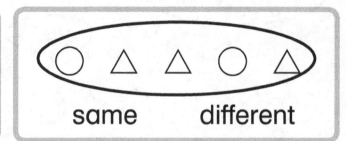
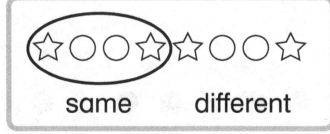

PA1-2 A Core that Ends the Way It Starts *(cont'd)*

☐ Circle the core.

Does the core end the way it starts?

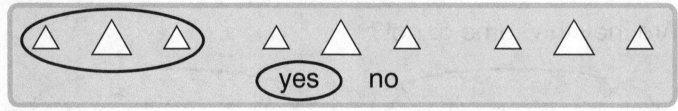

yes   no

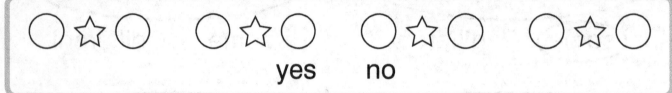

yes   no

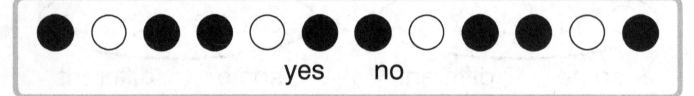

yes   no

2 3 4 2 2 3 4 2 2 3 4 2

yes   no

yes   no

yes   no

yes   no

PA1-2 A Core that Ends the Way It Starts *(cont'd)*

The core is circled.

☐ Extend the pattern.

(A B C) A B C A B _ _ _ _ _

(A B A) A B A _ _ _ _ _ _ _

(A B A A) A B A A _ _ _ _ _

(B A C B) _ _ _ _ _ _ _ _ _

(B A C) B _ _ _ _ _ _ _ _ _

(A A B) A A _ _ _ _ _ _ _ _

(A A B A) A _ _ _ _ _ _ _ _

PA1-3 Pattern Rules

☐ Circle the core.
☐ Describe the pattern.

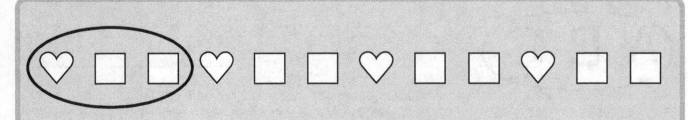

_____*heart*_____, _____*square*_____, _____*square*_____, then repeat

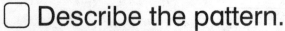

A B A B A B A B A B A B A B

_____, _____, then repeat

_____, _____, _____, then repeat

_____, _____, _____, then repeat

PA1-4 Showing Patterns in Different Ways

☐ Put the same letter under the same shape.

☐ ☐ △ ○ ☐ ☐ △ ○ ☐ ☐ △ ○

A A B C A A B C A A B C

☐ △ ☐ △ ☐ △

___ ___ ___ ___ ___ ___

○ △ ○ △ ○ △

___ ___ ___ ___ ___ ___

☐ ○ ☐ ☐ ○ ☐

___ ___ ___ ___ ___ ___

☐ △ ○ ☐ △ ○

___ ___ ___ ___ ___ ___

☐ △ ○ ○ ☐ △ ○ ○ ☐ △ ○ ○

___ ___ ___ ___ ___ ___ ___ ___ ___ ___ ___ ___

○ △ ☐ ○ ○ △ ☐ ○ ○ △ ☐ ○

___ ___ ___ ___ ___ ___ ___ ___ ___ ___ ___ ___

PA1-4 Showing Patterns in Different Ways (cont'd)

☐ Show the pattern in 2 ways.

Use 😊, ☹, 😐 and 1, 2, 3.

A	B	B	A	B	B	A	B	B
😊	☹	☹	😊	☹	☹	😊	☹	☹
_1_	_2_	_2_	_1_	_2_	_2_	_1_	_2_	_2_

A	B	C	A	B	C	A	B	C
😊	☹	😐	◯	◯	◯	◯	◯	◯
_1_	_2_	_3_	___	___	___	___	___	___

A	B	C	C	A	B	C	C	A	B	C	C
◯	◯	◯	◯	◯	◯	◯	◯	◯	◯	◯	◯

___

A	B	B	C	A	B	B	C	A	B	B	C
◯	◯	◯	◯	◯	◯	◯	◯	◯	◯	◯	◯

___

PA1-4 **Showing Patterns in Different Ways** *(cont'd)*

☐ Match the patterns.

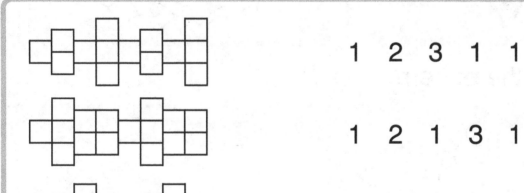

A B B A B B   ☹ ☹ ☺ ☹ ☹ ☺

A A B A A B   ☹ ☺ ☺ ☹ ☺ ☺

A B A A B A   ☺ ☹ ☺ ☺ ☹ ☺

A B C A B C   ☺ ☹ ☐ ☺ ☹ ☐

	1 2 3 1 1 2 3 1
	1 2 1 3 1 2 1 3
	1 3 2 2 1 3 2 2

Bonus: Match the core to the pattern.

A B C C

A A B B

A B C B

PA1-5 Problems and Puzzles

☐ Circle the core.

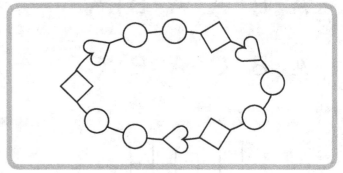

☐ Continue the pattern.

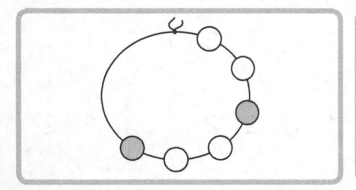

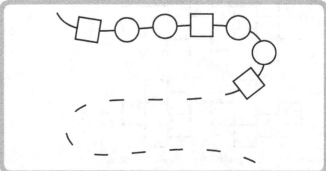

Bonus

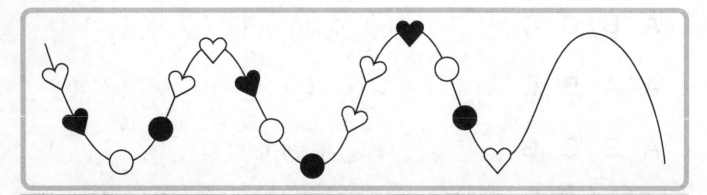

PA1-5 Problems and Puzzles *(continued)*

These are postal codes.

☐ Write **#** under numbers and **L** under letters.

M 2 N 7 H 4	L 6 B 5 N 8
— — — — — —	— — — — — —

V 5 T 1 Z 9	R 2 E 1 B 8
— — — — — —	— — — — — —

T 2 E 3 B 9	M 6 J 2 Z 4
— — — — — —	— — — — — —

M 6 N 3 E 3	**Bonus** B 0 E 3 O 9
— — — — — —	— — — — — —

☐ Circle the core of the repeating pattern.

UNIT 3

Measurement 1

ME1-1 The Distance Around

☐ Measure the distance around. Use string ∿ and cubes ▭ or tape ⊙ and marker ▭▬.

☐ Order the objects from longest distance around to shortest distance around.

table	wrist
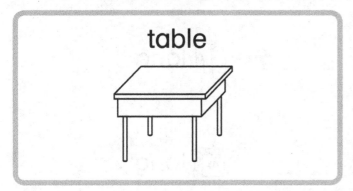	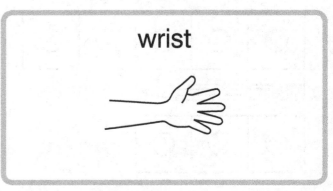
mug	book

rug	Choose your own.
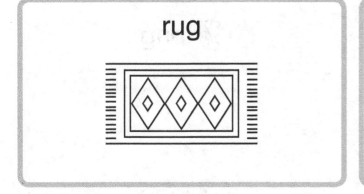	

1. _____ 4. _____

2. _____ 5. _____

3. _____ 6. _____

ME1-2 Measuring Length

☐ Colour the **longer** pencil.
☐ Circle the **larger** number.

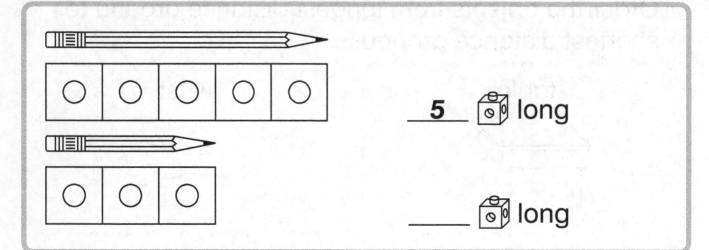

_**5**_ 🎲 long

_____ 🎲 long

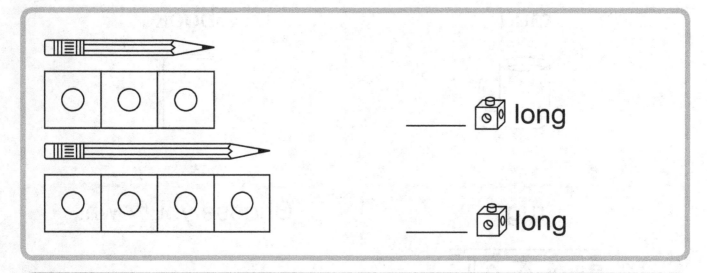

_____ 🎲 long

_____ 🎲 long

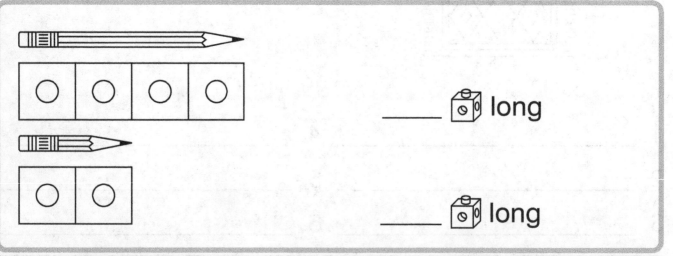

_____ 🎲 long

_____ 🎲 long

ME1-2 Measuring Length (continued)

☐ Colour the **longer** pencil.
☐ Circle the **larger** number.

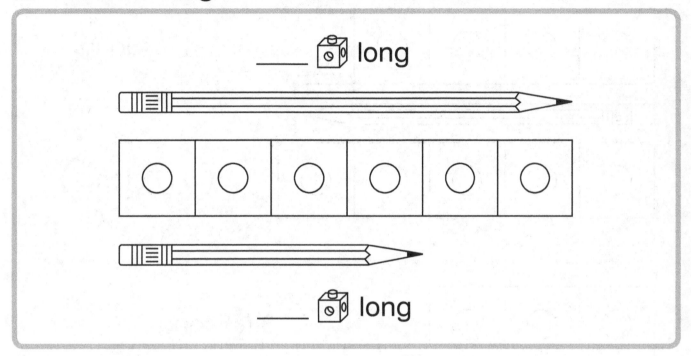

Whose pencil is **longer**?

Bilal 5 🎲 long	Tasfia 6 🎲 long
Liam 7 🎲 long	Carl 4 🎲 long

Dalion 9 🎲 long	Mariah 2 🎲 long
Ahmed 8 🎲 long	Calli 3 🎲 long

ME1-2 Measuring Length (continued)

The length is closer to…

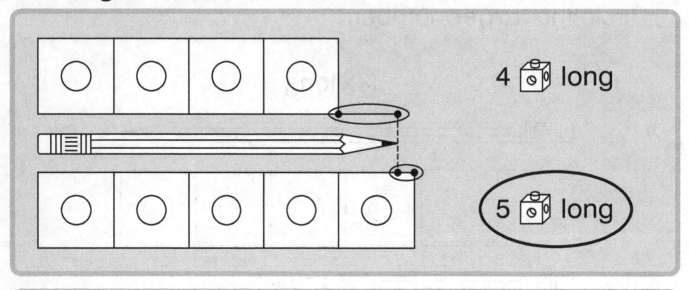

4 🎲 long

5 🎲 long

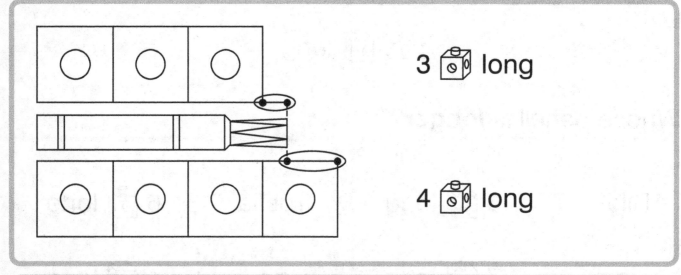

3 🎲 long

4 🎲 long

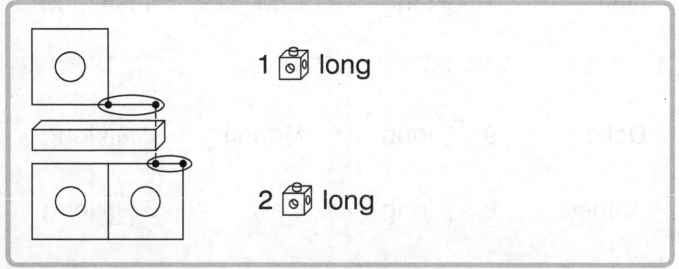

1 🎲 long

2 🎲 long

ME1-2 **Measuring Length** *(continued)*

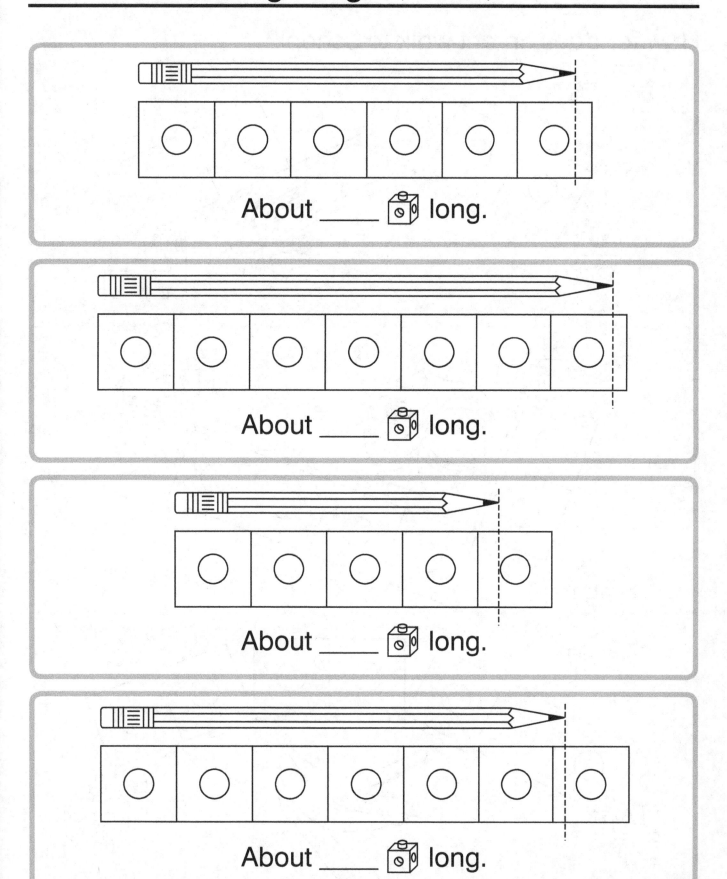

About _____ 🎲 long.

About _____ 🎲 long.

About _____ 🎲 long.

About _____ 🎲 long.

ME1-3 Length and Distance

How far does an ant walk to school?

6

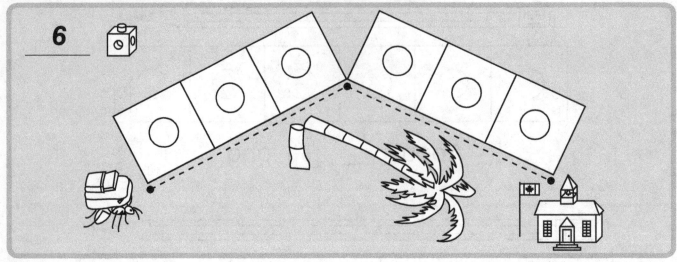

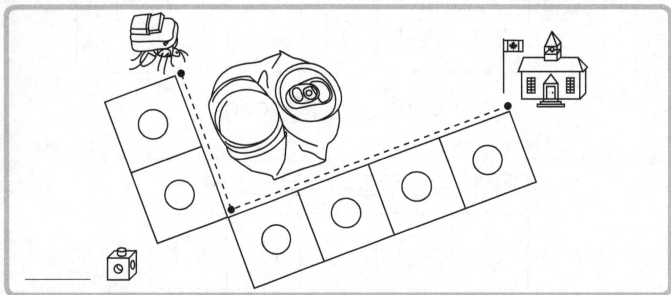

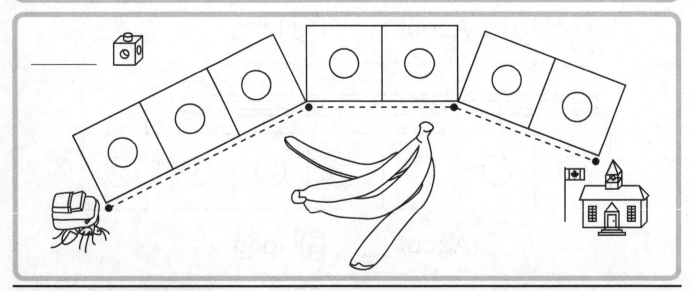

No unauthorized copying   **JUMP AT HOME GRADE 1**

UNIT 4

Probability and Data Management 1

PDM1-1 Sorting into Groups

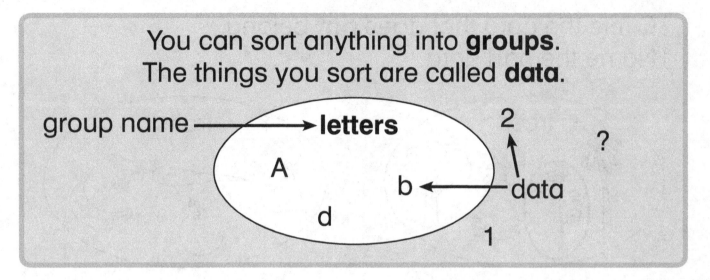

You can sort anything into **groups**.
The things you sort are called **data**.

group name ⟶ **letters**

A

b

d

2

?

data

1

☐ Sort the data.

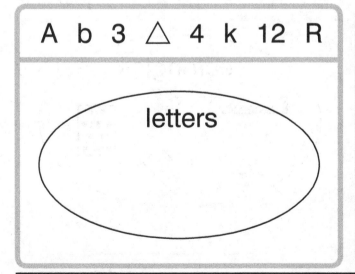

x̷ 5̷ ! E * 7 s

5

letters

t

E 3 7 s < 8 d 9

numbers

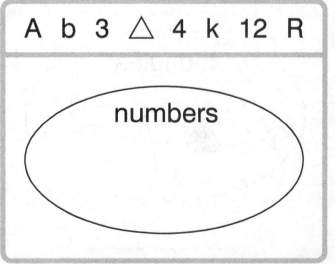

A b 3 △ 4 k 12 R

letters

A b 3 △ 4 k 12 R

numbers

PDM1-2 Does It Belong?

☐ Circle the data that does **not** belong.
☐ Name the odd data.

trees

flower

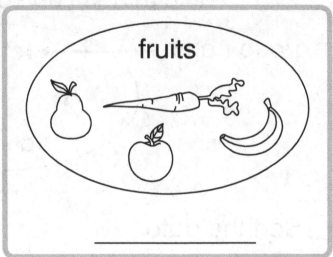

fruits

_____

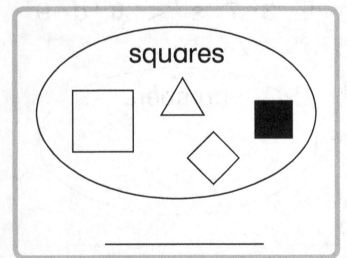

squares

_____

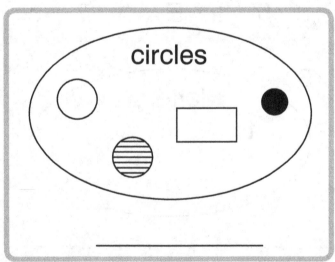

circles

_____

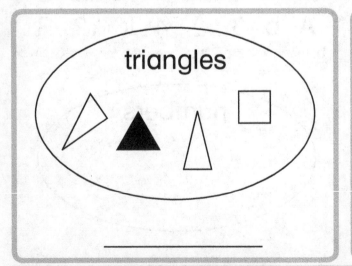

triangles

_____

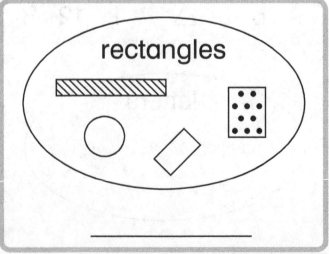

rectangles

_____

PDM1-3 Differences and Sorting

What changes?

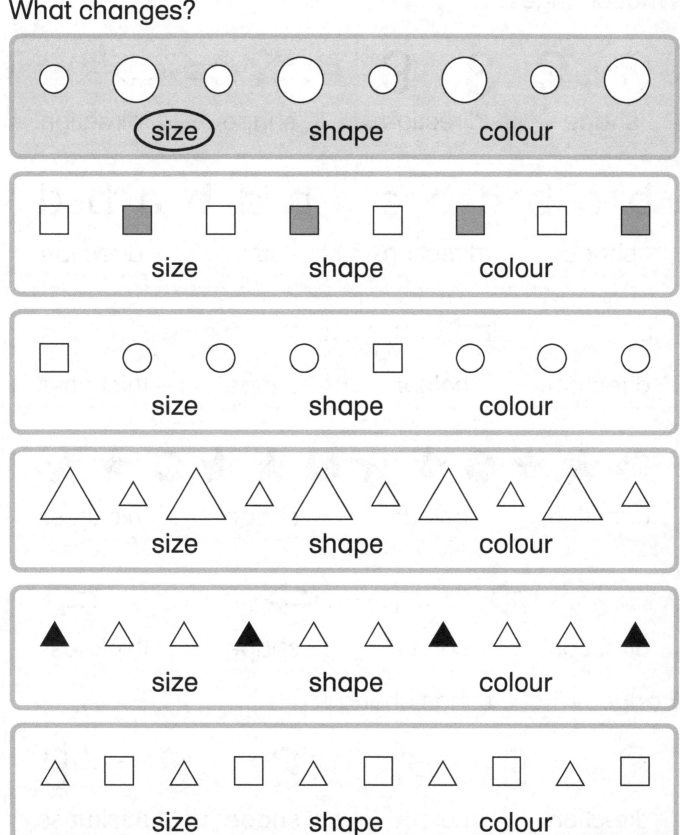

PDM1-3 **Differences and Sorting** (continued)

What changes?

3 3 3 3
shape   direction

⇒ ⇐ ⇒ ⇐
shape   direction

b c b c b c
shape   direction

b d b d b d
size   direction

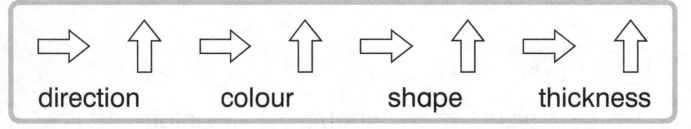
direction   colour   shape   thickness

●★★●★★●★★●★★
direction   colour   shape   thickness

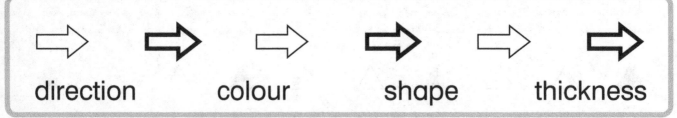
direction   colour   shape   thickness

Bonus: What 2 things change?

direction   colour   shape   thickness

PDM1-3 Differences and Sorting *(continued)*

☐ Find 3 differences.

sleeves	*short*	*long*
buttons	*no*	*yes*
colour	*dark*	*light*

number of sides	_____	_____
straight sides	_____	_____
colour	_____	_____

_____   _____   _____

_____   _____   _____

_____

No unauthorized copying

PDM1-3 Differences and Sorting (continued)

☐ Find 3 differences.

PDM1-3 **Differences and Sorting** *(continued)*

☐ Sort the words two ways.

me	on	yellow	red
blue	green	the	a

1.

more than
2 letters

fewer than
3 letters

me

2.

not colours

me

_____

PDM1-3 **Differences and Sorting** *(continued)*

☐ Sort the data two ways.

A 2 d m 6 R V 3 J + 5 7 ? c

1.

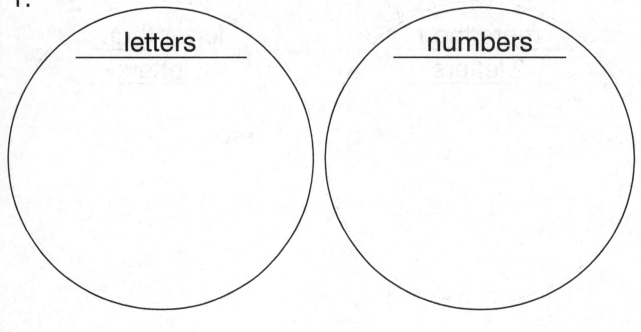

letters   numbers

2.

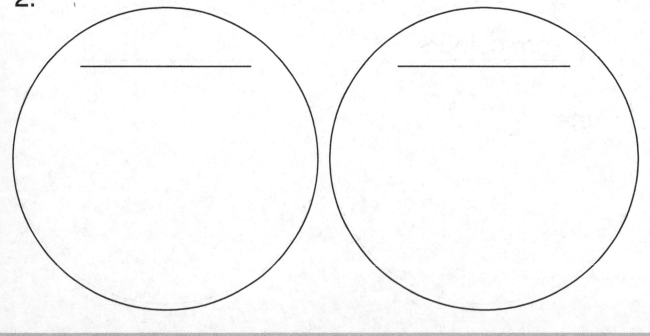

PDM1-4 **Sorting Rules**

☐ Find one word that describes the data.

_____*shirts*_____

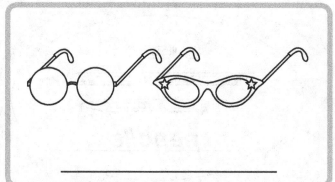

_____

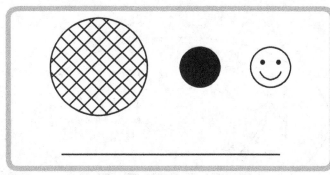

_____

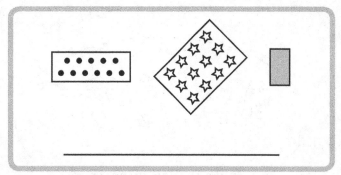

_____

_____

_____

☐ Find two words that describe the data.

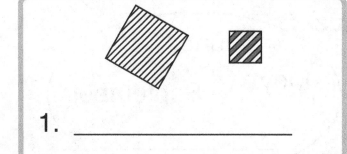

1. _____
2. _____

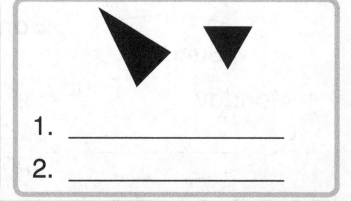

1. _____
2. _____

PDM1-5 Sorting Rules — Many Groups

How were these sorted?

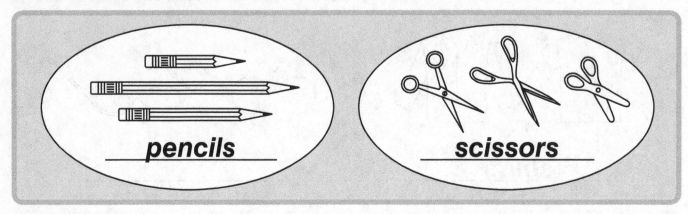

_____pencils_____   _____scissors_____

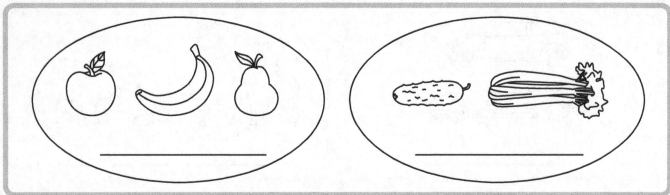

_____   _____

_____   _____

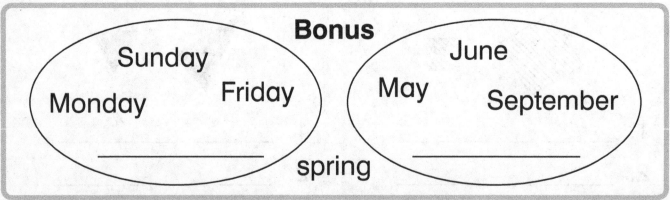

Bonus

Sunday

Monday   Friday

June

May   September

_____   _____

spring

UNIT 5

Number Sense 2

NS1-23 Reading Number Words (Zero to Ten)

☐ Match the word with the number.

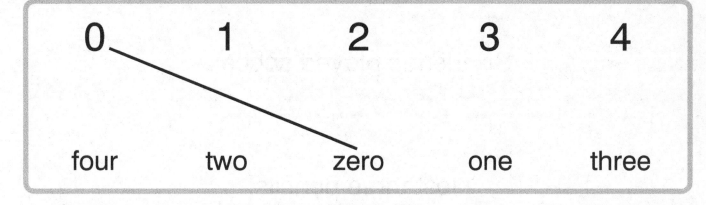

0	1	2	3	4
four	two	zero	one	three

5	6	7	8	9
seven	eight	nine	five	six

2	4	6	8	10
four	eight	two	ten	six

5	7	2	9	3
three	two	nine	seven	five

NS1-23 **Reading Number Words (Zero to Ten)** *(cont'd)*

☐ Write the number above the number word.

6
Six friends played soccer.

I lost three pencils.

The girl is five years old.

There are seven colours in the rainbow.

The boy has eight crayons and four markers.

The class has one teacher, two tutors,

six girls, and one boy.

NS1-24 Writing Number Words to Ten

How many balloons?

☐ Trace the right word.

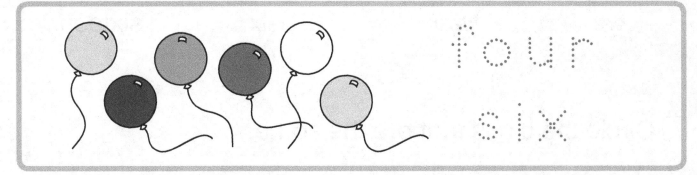

four

six

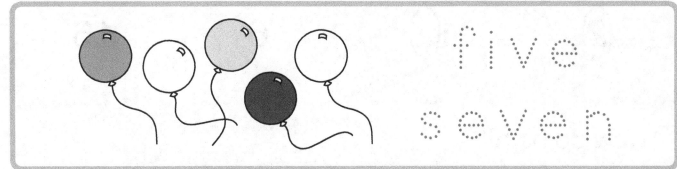

five

seven

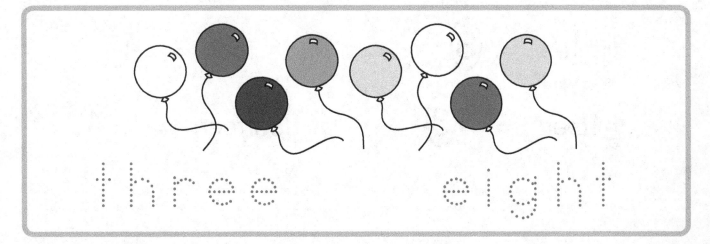

three   eight

two

ten

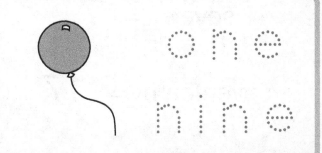

one

nine

NS1-25 **Reading Number Words to Twenty**

☐ Underline the beginning letters that are the same.

<u>tw</u>o <u>tw</u>elve	six sixteen

☐ Circle the digits that are the same.

② 1②	6 16

☐ Now do both!

<u>th</u>ree = ③ <u>th</u>irteen = 1③	four = 4 fourteen = 14
seven = 7 seventeen = 17	five = 5 fifteen = 15

NS1-25 **Reading Number Words to Twenty** *(cont'd)*

☐ Match by the first 2 letters.

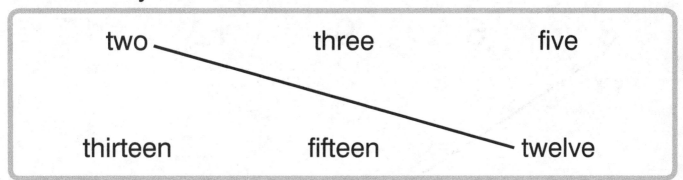

☐ Write the numbers.

nineteen = __1__ __9__

sixteen = __1__ ____

eighteen = __1__ ____

twelve = __1__ ____

thirteen = ____ ____

fifteen = ____ ____

sixteen = ____ ____

seventeen = ____ ____

fourteen = ____ ____

Bonus

eleven = ____ ____

NS1-25 Reading Number Words to Twenty *(cont'd)*

☐ Match the word with the number.

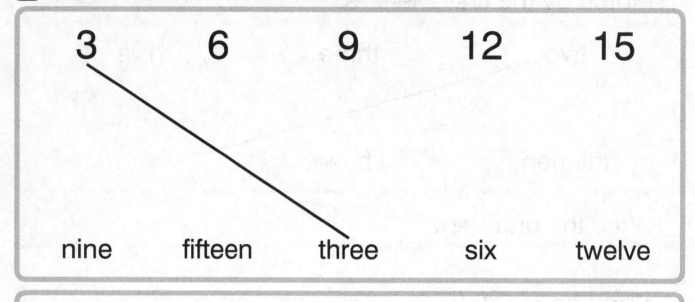

3	6	9	12	15

nine	fifteen	three	six	twelve

0	4	8	12	16

eight	zero	sixteen	four	twelve

11	13	15	17	19

fifteen	nineteen	thirteen	eleven	seventeen

NS1-25 Reading Number Words to Twenty *(cont'd)*

☐ Write the number above the number word.

13

Dara is thirteen years old.

Sixteen friends played soccer.

I have twenty teeth.

We played ball for fifteen minutes.

Sara has eleven pencil crayons.

Bonus

Naima's soccer team has twelve players —

seven girls and five boys.

NS1-26 What Comes Next?

☐ Write the missing numbers.

33	34	35		37
43	44	45	46	47
53	54	55	56	57

11	12	13	14
21	22	23	24
31		33	34

21	22	23
31	32	33
41	42	
51	52	53

64	65	66
	75	76
84	85	86
94	95	

48	49
58	59
	69
78	79

16	17	18	19	20
26	27	28	29	30
36		38	39	40
46	47	48	49	
56	57	58	59	60

Bonus

32		34	35	
42	43	44		46
	53	54	55	56
62	63	64	65	
72	73		75	76

NS1-27 Ordering Numbers to 50

☐ Shade the numbers.
☐ Write them in order.

13   6   11

1	2	3	4
5	6	7	8
9	10	11	12
13	14	15	16

___6___ ___11___ ___13___

35   28   40

25	26	27	28
29	30	31	32
33	34	35	36
37	38	39	40

_____ _____ _____

47   30   39   22   48   60   54

21	22	23	24	25	26	27	28	29	30
31	32	33	34	35	36	37	38	39	40
41	42	43	44	45	46	47	48	49	50
51	52	53	54	55	56	57	58	59	60

_____ _____ _____ _____ _____ _____ _____

NS1-28 Addition Word Problems

☐ Add. Use the pictures to help you.

3 flowers   2 more flowers

3 + 2 = ☐

5 flowers   3 more flowers

5 + 3 = ☐

4 flowers   4 more flowers

4 + 4 = ☐

3 flowers   6 more flowers

3 + 6 = ☐

NS1-28 Addition Word Problems *(continued)*

☐ Write the number above the number word.
☐ Draw a picture to add.
☐ Write the number sentence.

2	7
two trees	seven more trees

$$\boxed{2} + \boxed{7} = \boxed{9}$$

---

five pencils   four more pencils

$$\boxed{} + \boxed{} = \boxed{}$$

---

six baseballs   five more baseballs

$$\boxed{} + \boxed{} = \boxed{}$$

NS1-28 Addition Word Problems (continued)

☐ Draw circles to help you add.

3 flies were buzzing.   2 joined them.

How many flies in total?

3 + 2 = | 5 |

Sue has 4 cats.   John has 2 cats.

How many cats altogether?

4 + 2 = ☐

Finn has **five** oranges.   Pam has **three** oranges.

How many oranges altogether?

☐ + ☐ = ☐

Sonia has four fish.   Tom has four fish.

How many fish altogether?

☐ + ☐ = ☐

NS1-28 **Addition Word Problems** *(continued)*

☐ Draw circles to solve the problem.

There are five small turtles.

There are six big turtles.

How many turtles are there altogether?

☐ + ☐ = ☐

Eight children were playing soccer.

Five children joined them.

How many are playing soccer now?

☐ + ☐ = ☐

There are seven big tables.

There are six small tables.

How many tables are there altogether?

☐ + ☐ = ☐

NS1-29 Subtraction Word Problems

☐ Draw a picture to subtract.

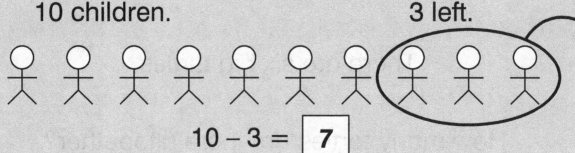

10 children.   3 left.

$$10 - 3 = \boxed{7}$$

---

12 children.   5 went away.

$$12 - 5 = \boxed{}$$

---

9 children.   6 left.

$$9 - 6 = \boxed{}$$

---

13 children.   5 went away.

$$13 - 5 = \boxed{}$$

NS1-29 Subtraction Word Problems (continued)

☐ Draw circles to subtract.

10 flies were buzzing.

A frog ate 4 of them.

⊗ ⊗ ⊗ ⊗ ○ ○ ○ ○ ○ ○

How many are left? ___6___

Eight children were playing soccer.

Four left to go skipping.

How many are still playing soccer? _____

Lee had twelve crayons.

Miki took away three of them.

How many does Lee have left? _____

Jacob has nine balloons.

Eight popped.

How many are left? _____

NS1-29 Subtraction Word Problems (continued)

☐ Write the subtraction sentence.
How many more or longer?

There are eight apples. | **8**

There are five pears. | **– 5**

There are ___*three*___ more apples than pears. | **3**

There are nine footballs. | ☐

There are four soccer balls. | **–** ☐

There are _____ more footballs. | ☐

Calli's pencil is five ☐ long. | ☐

Ron's pencil is two ☐ long. | **–** ☐

Calli's pencil is _____ ☐ longer than Ron's. | ☐

Pat's pencil is four ⊂⊃ long. | ☐

Bilal's pencil is three ⊂⊃ long. | **–** ☐

Pat's pencil is _____ ⊂⊃ longer than Bilal's. | ☐

NS1-30 Adding or Subtracting

Do the words **in bold** make you think of **+** or **−** ?

Three more **joined**. __+__	She **took** five **away**. _____
Four cookies are **left**. _____	How many **altogether**? _____
How many **in total**? _____	How many are **not** red? _____
Two children **left** to play. _____	How much **longer**? _____

She has three red marbles **and** two blue marbles.

_____

How many **more** apples **than** oranges are there?

_____

NS1-30 Adding or Subtracting (continued)

☐ Read the problem.
☐ Circle the correct way to find the answer.

Kim has five bananas. She ate three bananas. How many bananas are **left**?	5 + 3 ⬭(5 − 3)
There are five big pencils. There are two little pencils. How many pencils are there **altogether**?	5 + 2 5 − 2
There are three worms. The fish ate two worms. How many worms are **left**?	3 + 2 3 − 2
There are four red balloons. There are three blue balloons. How many balloons are there **altogether**?	4 + 3 4 − 3
Sonia has seven crayons. Five of them are red. How many are **not** red?	7 + 5 7 − 5

NS1-30 Adding or Subtracting *(continued)*

Do you add or subtract?

☐ Write the number sentence for the problem.

Aza has ten crayons. | Four of them are blue. | How many are not blue?

10 (**–**) **4** (**=**) **6**

Soren has four red crayons. | He has three blue crayons. | How many crayons does he have altogether?

☐ ◯ ☐ ◯ ☐

There are two big balloons. | There are seven small balloons. | How many balloons are there in total?

☐ ◯ ☐ ◯ ☐

There are five balloons. | Two of them are yellow. | How many balloons are not yellow?

☐ ◯ ☐ ◯ ☐

NS1-31 Adding Using a Chart

☐ Add.

$$\boxed{1}\ \boxed{2}\ \boxed{3}\ ④\ ⑤\ ⑥\ ⑦\ 8\ 9\ 10$$

$$3 + 4 = \rule{2cm}{0.4pt}$$

$$\boxed{1}\ \boxed{2}\ ③\ ④\ ⑤\ ⑥\ ⑦\ ⑧\ ⑨\ 10$$

$$2 + 7 = \rule{2cm}{0.4pt}$$

$$\boxed{1}\ \boxed{2}\ \boxed{3}\ \boxed{4}\ \boxed{5}\ \boxed{6}\ ⑦\ ⑧\ 9\ 10$$

$$6 + 2 = \rule{2cm}{0.4pt}$$

$$\boxed{1}\ \boxed{2}\ \boxed{3}\ \boxed{4}\ \boxed{5}\ \boxed{6}\ \boxed{7}\ \boxed{8}\ \boxed{9}\ ⑩$$
$$⑪\ ⑫\ 13\ 14\ 15\ 16\ 17\ 18\ 19\ 20$$

$$9 + 3 = \rule{2cm}{0.4pt}$$

$$\boxed{1}\ \boxed{2}\ \boxed{3}\ \boxed{4}\ \boxed{5}\ \boxed{6}\ \boxed{7}\ \boxed{8}\ ⑨\ ⑩$$
$$⑪\ ⑫\ ⑬\ 14\ 15\ 16\ 17\ 18\ 19\ 20$$

$$8 + 5 = \rule{2cm}{0.4pt}$$

NS1-31 Adding Using a Chart

NS1-31 Adding Using a Chart (continued)

☐ Shade the first number of squares.
☐ Circle the second number of squares.
☐ Add.

| 1 | 2 | 3 | ④ | ⑤ | ⑥ | ⑦ | ⑧ | 9 | 10 |

$$3 + 5 = \underline{\quad 8 \quad}$$

| 1 | 2 | 3 | 4 | 5 | 6 | 7 | 8 | 9 | 10 |

$$4 + 5 = \underline{\qquad}$$

| 1 | 2 | 3 | 4 | 5 | 6 | 7 | 8 | 9 | 10 |

$$8 + 1 = \underline{\qquad}$$

| 1 | 2 | 3 | 4 | 5 | 6 | 7 | 8 | 9 | 10 |

$$7 + 3 = \underline{\qquad}$$

| 1 | 2 | 3 | 4 | 5 | 6 | 7 | 8 | 9 | 10 |
| 11 | 12 | 13 | 14 | 15 | 16 | 17 | 18 | 19 | 20 |

$$12 + 6 = \underline{\qquad}$$

NS1-31 Adding Using a Chart *(continued)*

The square showing the first number is shaded.

☐ Add by circling the next 3 numbers.

| 1 | 2 | 3 | 4 | **5** | ⑥ | ⑦ | ⑧ | 9 | 10 |

$$5 + 3 = \underline{\ \textbf{8}\ }$$

| 1 | 2 | 3 | 4 | 5 | 6 | 7 | 8 | **9** | ⑩ |
| ⑪ | ⑫ | 13 | 14 | 15 | 16 | 17 | 18 | 19 | 20 |

$$9 + 3 = \underline{\qquad}$$

1	2	3	4	5
6	7	8	9	10
11	12	**13**	14	15
16	17	18	19	20

$$13 + 3 = \underline{\qquad}$$

1	2	3	4	5
6	7	8	9	10
11	12	13	14	**15**
16	17	18	19	20

$$15 + 3 = \underline{\qquad}$$

NS1-31 Adding Using a Chart *(continued)*

☐ Shade the square showing the first number.
☐ Circle the second number of squares.
☐ Add.

1	2	3	4	**5**	⑥	⑦	8	9	10

$$5 + 2 = \underline{\ 7\ }$$

1	2	3	4	5	6	7	8	9	10

$$7 + 3 = \underline{\qquad}$$

1	2	3	4	5	6	7	8	9	10
11	12	13	14	15	16	17	18	19	20

$$8 + 5 = \underline{\qquad}$$

1	2	3	4	5
6	7	8	9	10
11	12	13	14	15

$$4 + 7 = \underline{\qquad}$$

1	2	3	4	5
6	7	8	9	10
11	12	13	14	15

$$9 + 5 = \underline{\qquad}$$

NS1-32 Counting On to Add 1 or 2

☐ Colour the **next** circle.
☐ Add 1.

1   2   3   4

● ● ● ○

3 + 1 = ___4___

1   2   3   4   5

● ● ● ● ○

4 + 1 = _____

1   2   3

● ● ○

2 + 1 = _____

1   2   3   4   5   6

● ● ● ● ● ○

5 + 1 = _____

1   2   3   4   5   6   7   8   9   10

● ● ● ● ● ● ● ○

7 + 1 = _____

1   2   3   4   5   6   7   8   9   10

● ● ● ● ● ● ● ● ○

8 + 1 = _____

NS1-32 Counting On to Add 1 or 2 (continued)

◻ Find the **next** number.
◻ Add 1.

1   2   3   **4**   5

4 + 1 = __5__

1   2   **3**   4   5

3 + 1 = _____

1 2 3 4 **5** 6 7

5 + 1 = _____

1 2 3 4 5 **6** 7

6 + 1 = _____

1   2   3   4   5   6   7   8   9   10

7 + 1 = _____

1   2   3   4   5   6   7   8   9   10

9 + 1 = _____

1+1= __

2+1= __

8+1= __

Bonus

14+1= __

NS1-32 Counting On to Add 1 or 2 *(continued)*

☐ Find the **next** 2 numbers.
☐ Add 2.

1 2 3 **4** 5 6 7

4 + 2 = __6__

1 2 **3** 4 5 6 7

3 + 2 = _____

1 2 3 4 5 **6** 7 8

6 + 2 = _____

1 2 3 4 **5** 6 7 8

5 + 2 = _____

1 2 3 4 5 6 7 8 9 10 11 12

8 + 2 = _____

1 2 3 4 5 6 7 8 9 10 11 12

9 + 2 = _____

7 + 2 = ___

2 + 2 = ___

10 + 2 = ___

Bonus
17 + 2 = ___

NS1-33 Counting On to Add

☐ Add by counting on.

5   __6__   __7__

5 + 2 = __7__

4   _____   _____   _____

4 + 3 = _____

6   _____   _____   _____   _____

6 + 4 = _____

7   _____   _____   _____   _____

7 + 4 = _____

8   _____   _____

8 + 2 = _____

5 + 2 = _____

3 + 5 = _____

7 + 3 = _____

NS1-33 **Counting On to Add** (continued)

There are **5** apples in the bag.
☐ Add by counting on.

5 + 3 = ___**8**___

5 + 4 = _____

5 + 2 = _____

5 + 5 = _____

5 + 1 = _____

5 + 6 = _____

No unauthorized copying   **JUMP AT HOME GRADE 1**

NS1-34 Counting On in Two Ways

☐ Add by counting on in two ways.

$7 + 3 = \underline{\textit{10}}$

7   <u>*8*</u>   <u>*9*</u>   <u>*10*</u>

3   <u>*4*</u>   <u>*5*</u>   <u>*6*</u>   <u>*7*</u>   <u>*8*</u>   <u>*9*</u>   <u>*10*</u>

$4 + 8 = \underline{\hspace{1.5cm}}$

4   ___ ___ ___ ___ ___ ___ ___ ___

8   ___ ___ ___ ___

$11 + 2 = \underline{\hspace{1.5cm}}$

11   ___ ___

2   ___ ___ ___ ___ ___ ___ ___ ___ ___ ___ ___

$3 + 10 = \underline{\hspace{1.5cm}}$

3   ___ ___ ___ ___ ___ ___ ___ ___ ___ ___

10   ___ ___ ___

NS1-34 Counting On in Two Ways (continued)

☐ Draw the correct number of blanks.
☐ Add by counting on in two ways.

$2 + 5 =$ __7__

2 __3__ __4__ __5__ __6__ __7__
5 __6__ __7__

$7 + 4 =$ _____

7
4

$3 + 9 =$ _____

3
9

☐ Fill in the blanks.

Counting on from the _____ number
bigger / smaller
is easier because there are _____
numbers to count.
more / fewer

NS1-35 Using Number Lines to Add

The frog takes 2 leaps.
Where does he end up?

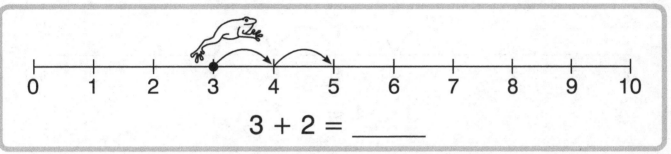

3 + 2 = _____

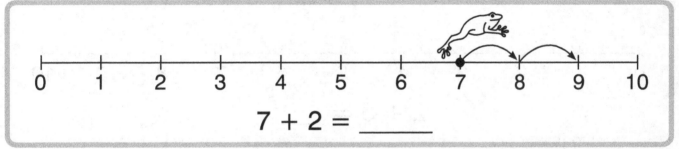

7 + 2 = _____

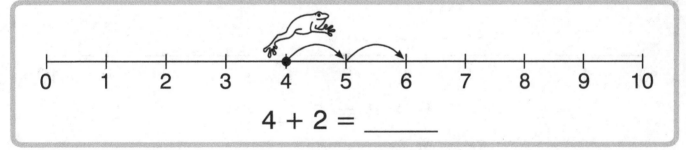

4 + 2 = _____

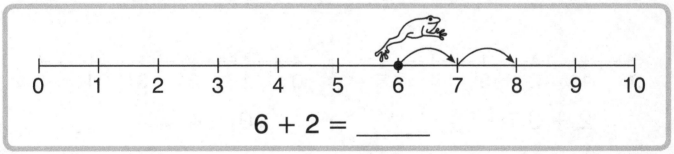

6 + 2 = _____

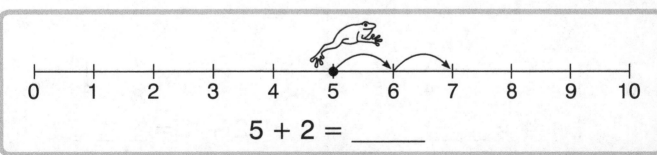

5 + 2 = _____

NS1-35 Using Number Lines to Add (continued)

☐ Trace the leaps.
☐ Add.

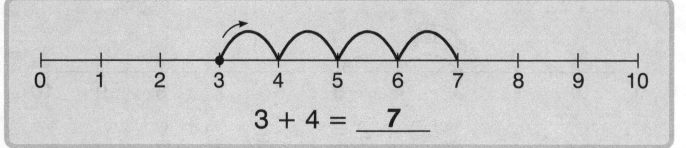

3 + 4 = ___7___

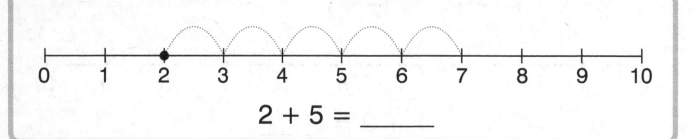

2 + 5 = _____

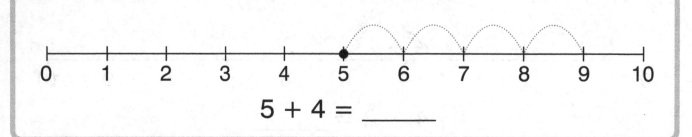

5 + 4 = _____

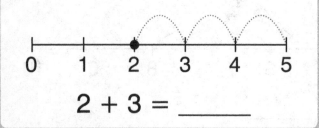

2 + 3 = _____

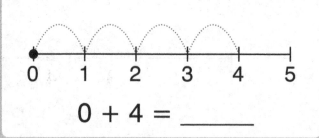

0 + 4 = _____

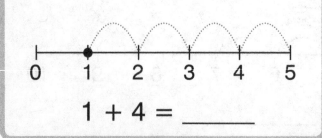

1 + 4 = _____

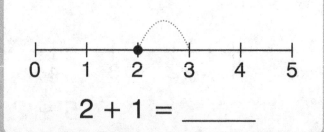

2 + 1 = _____

NS1-35 Using Number Lines to Add *(continued)*

☐ Match the dots to the addition sentence.

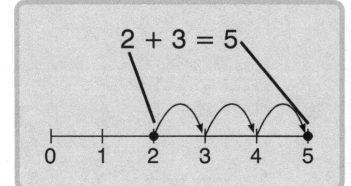

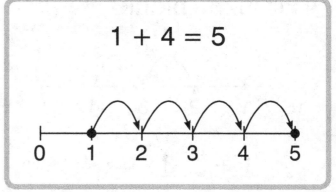

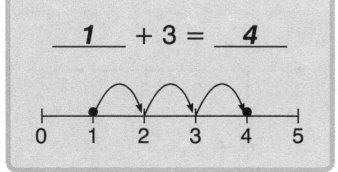

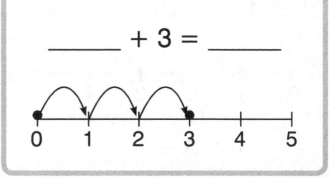

☐ Fill in the blanks.

$$\underline{\,\,1\,\,} + 3 = \underline{\,\,4\,\,}$$

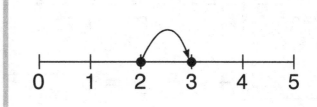

$$\underline{\hspace{1cm}} + 3 = \underline{\hspace{1cm}}$$

$$\underline{\hspace{1cm}} + 1 = \underline{\hspace{1cm}}$$

$$\underline{\hspace{1cm}} + 2 = \underline{\hspace{1cm}}$$

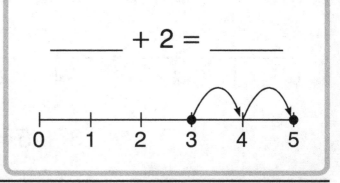

NS1-35 Using Number Lines to Add *(continued)*

☐ Count the leaps.
☐ Fill in the blank.

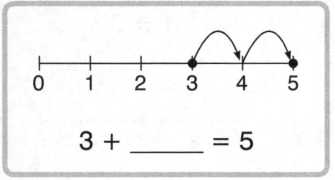

1 + __*3*__ = 4

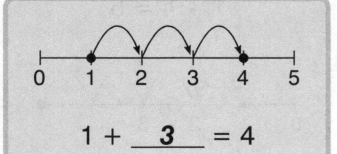

2 + _____ = 3

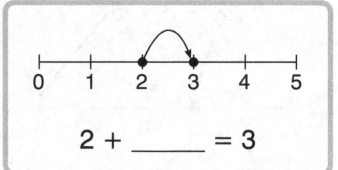

3 + _____ = 5

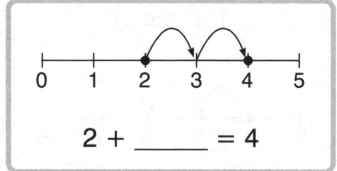

2 + _____ = 4

☐ Trace the correct number of leaps.
☐ Add.

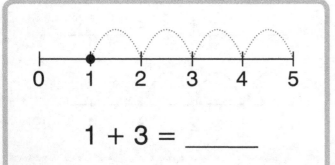

1 + 3 = _____

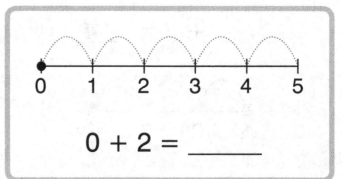

0 + 2 = _____

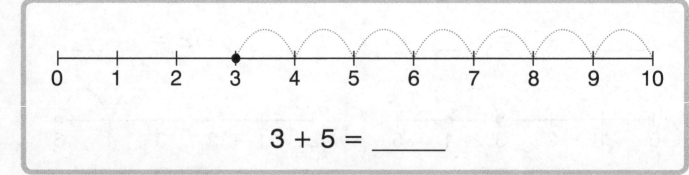

3 + 5 = _____

NS1-35 Using Number Lines to Add *(continued)*

☐ Use a number line to add.

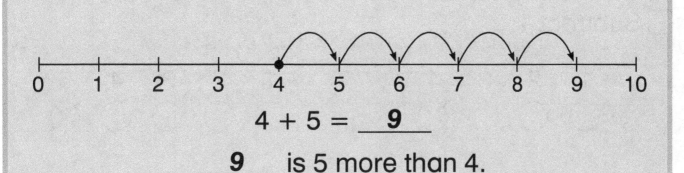

4 + 5 = __9__

__9__ is 5 more than 4.

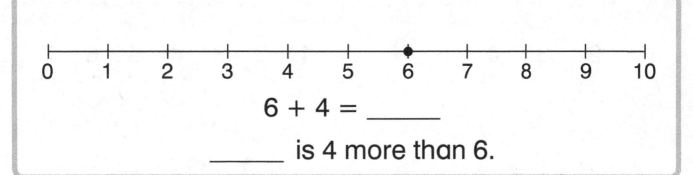

6 + 4 = _____

_____ is 4 more than 6.

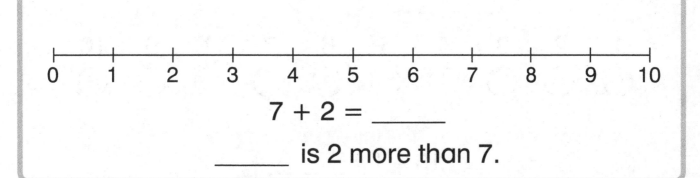

7 + 2 = _____

_____ is 2 more than 7.

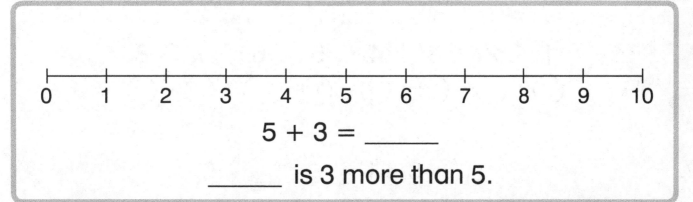

5 + 3 = _____

_____ is 3 more than 5.

NS1-36 Subtracting 1 or 2

☐ Take away the last circle.
☐ Subtract 1.

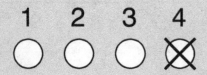

$4 - 1 =$ ___3___

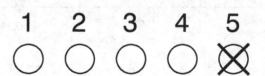

$5 - 1 =$ _____

1 2 3 4 5 6
○ ○ ○ ○ ○ ○

$6 - 1 =$ _____

1 2 3 4 5 6 7
○ ○ ○ ○ ○ ○ ○

$7 - 1 =$ _____

1 2 3 4 5 6 7 8 9 10
○ ○ ○ ○ ○ ○ ○ ○ ○ ○

$10 - 1 =$ _____

1 2 3 4 5 6 7 8
○ ○ ○ ○ ○ ○ ○ ○

$8 - 1 =$ _____

NS1-36 **Subtracting 1 or 2** (continued)

☐ Draw 1 leap back.
☐ Subtract 1.

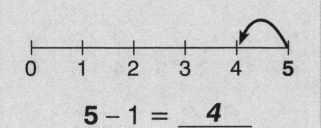

$5 - 1 =$ ___4___

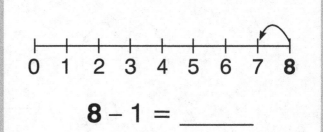

$8 - 1 =$ _____

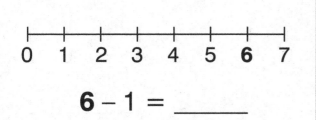

$6 - 1 =$ _____

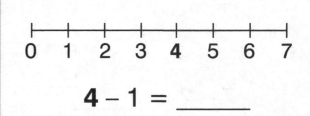

$4 - 1 =$ _____

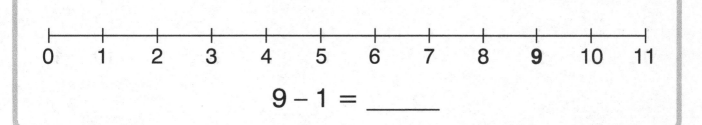

$9 - 1 =$ _____

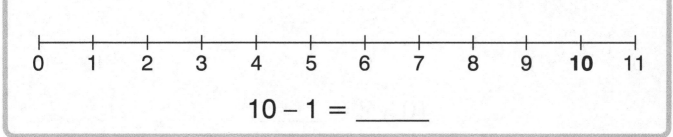

$10 - 1 =$ _____

☐ Subtract.

			Bonus
$3 - 1 =$ ___	$7 - 1 =$ ___	$11 - 1 =$ ___	$14 - 1 =$ ___

NS1-36 Subtracting 1 or 2 (continued)

☐ Draw 2 leaps back.
☐ Subtract 2.

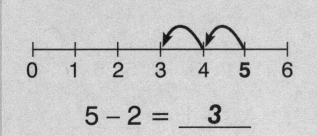

$5 - 2 =$ __3__

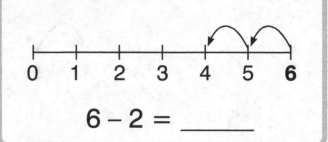

$6 - 2 =$ _____

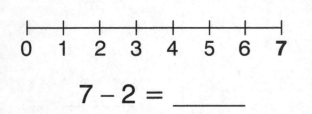

$7 - 2 =$ _____

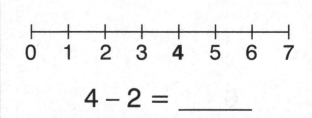

$4 - 2 =$ _____

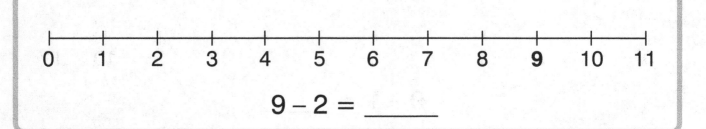

$9 - 2 =$ _____

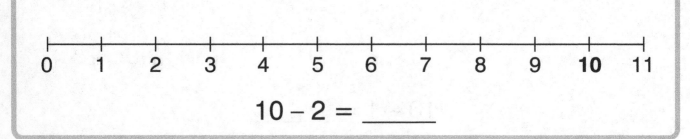

$10 - 2 =$ _____

☐ Subtract.

$3 - 2 =$ ___ $8 - 2 =$ ___ $11 - 2 =$ ___

Bonus
$15 - 2 =$ ___

NS1-37 Using Number Lines to Subtract

☐ Trace the leaps. Start at the big dot.
☐ Count the leaps.

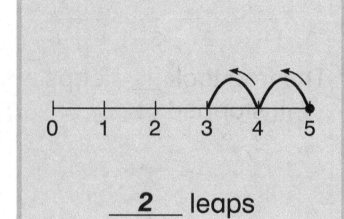

___**2**___ leaps

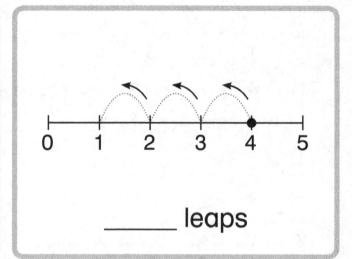

_____ leaps

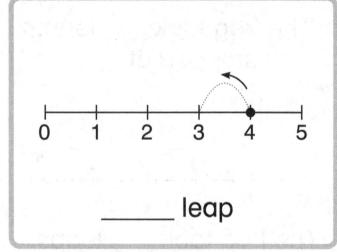

_____ leap

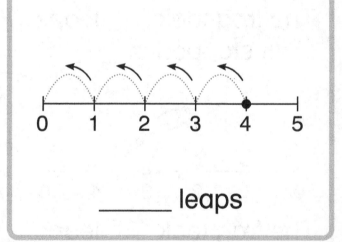

_____ leaps

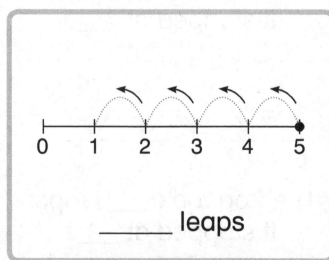

_____ leaps

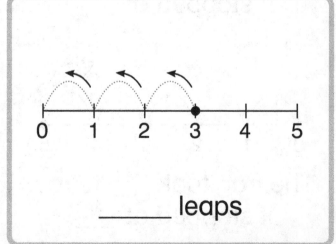

_____ leaps

No unauthorized copying

NS1-37 Using Number Lines to Subtract (continued)

☐ Fill in the blanks.

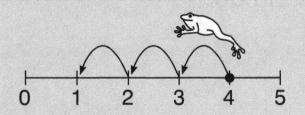

The frog took __3__ leaps.
It stopped at __1__.

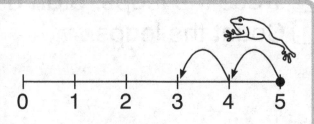

The frog took ___ leaps.
It stopped at ___.

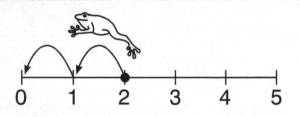

The frog took ___ leaps.
It stopped at ___.

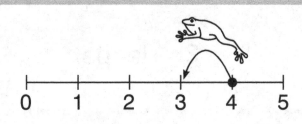

The frog took ___ leap.
It stopped at ___.

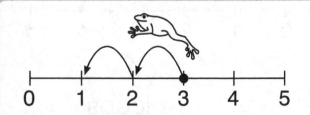

The frog took ___ leaps.
It stopped at ___.

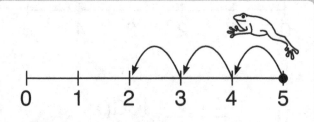

The frog took ___ leaps.
It stopped at ___.

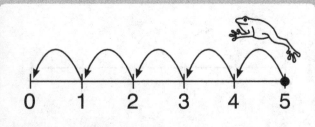

The frog took ___ leaps.
It stopped at ___.

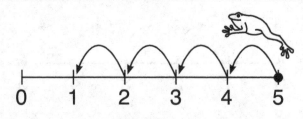

The frog took ___ leaps.
It stopped at ___.

NS1-37 Using Number Lines to Subtract *(continued)*

The frog took 2 leaps backwards.

☐ Trace the 2 leaps.
What number did the frog stop at?

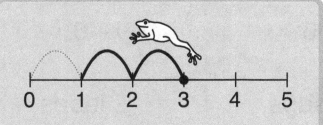

The frog stopped at __*1*__.

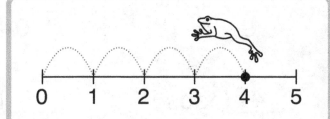

The frog stopped at ____.

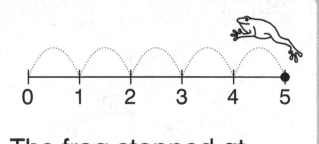

The frog stopped at ____.

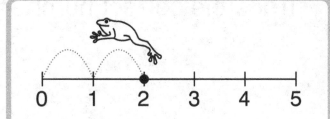

The frog stopped at ____.

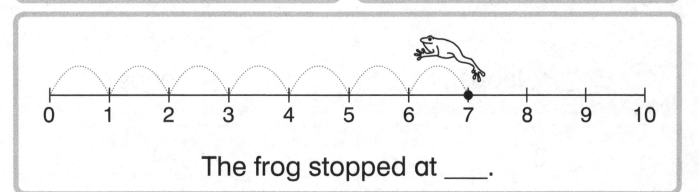

The frog stopped at ____.

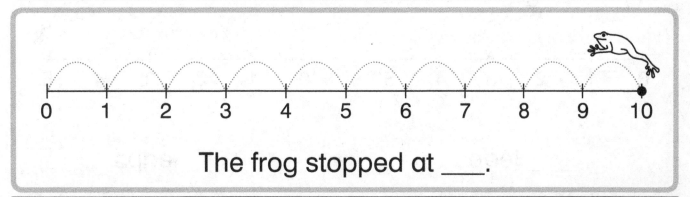

The frog stopped at ____.

NS1-37 Using Number Lines to Subtract *(continued)*

The frog starts at 9.
How many leaps should the frog take?

9 – 4	9 – 3	9 – 6
4 leaps	___ leaps	___ leaps

☐ How many leaps should the frog take?
Trace the correct number of leaps.

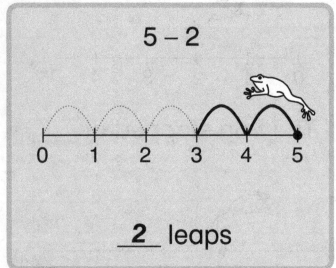

5 – 2

2 leaps

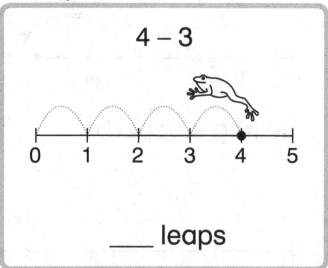

4 – 3

___ leaps

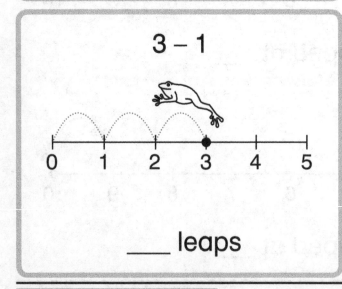

3 – 1

___ leaps

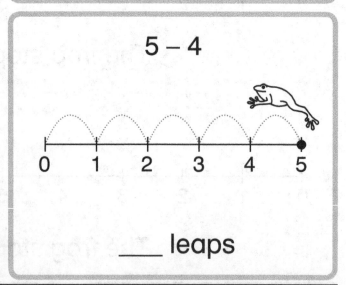

5 – 4

___ leaps

NS1-37 Using Number Lines to Subtract (continued)

☐ Trace 4 leaps back. Start at the big dot.
☐ Subtract 4.

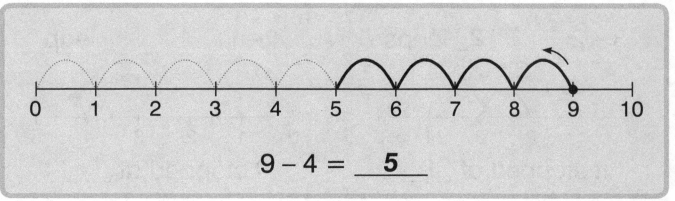

$$9 - 4 = \underline{\quad 5 \quad}$$

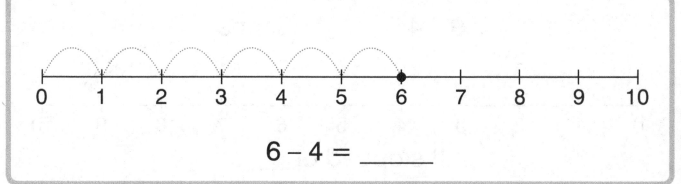

$$7 - 4 = \underline{\qquad}$$

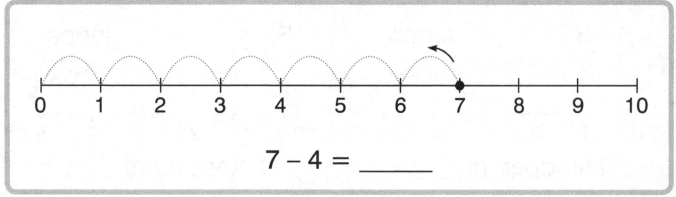

$$6 - 4 = \underline{\qquad}$$

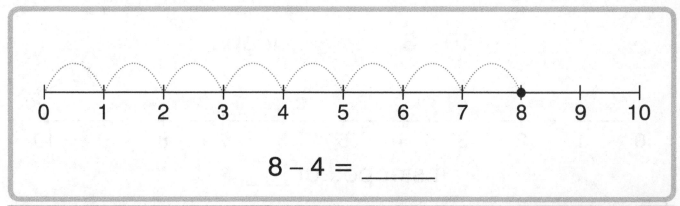

$$8 - 4 = \underline{\qquad}$$

NS1-37 **Using Number Lines to Subtract** (continued)

☐ Trace the correct number of leaps. Start at the big dot.
☐ Fill in the blanks.

3 − 2   __2__ leaps

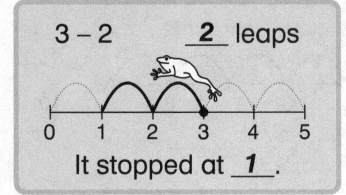

It stopped at _1_.

4 − 1   ___ leap

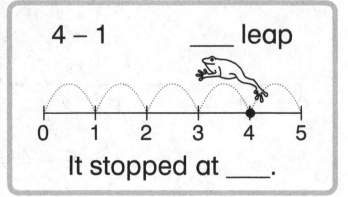

It stopped at ___.

5 − 3   ___ leaps

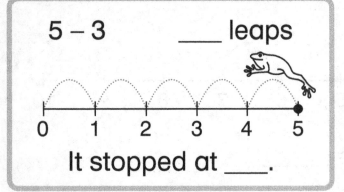

It stopped at ___.

5 − 4   ___ leaps

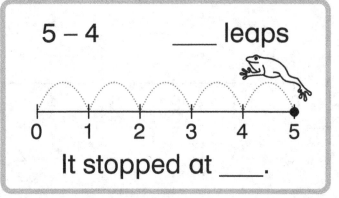

It stopped at ___.

9 − 4   ___ leaps

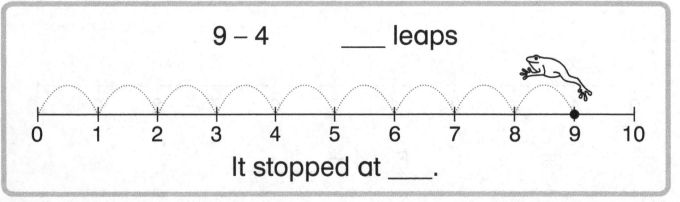

It stopped at ___.

10 − 3   ___ leaps

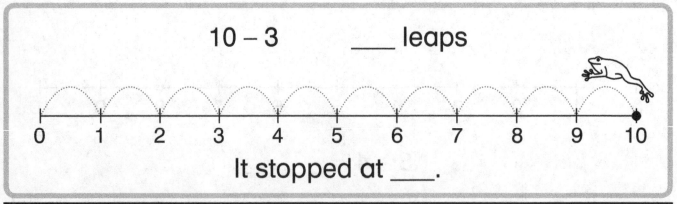

It stopped at ___.

NS1-37 Using Number Lines to Subtract *(continued)*

☐ Trace the correct number of leaps back.
Start at the big dot.
☐ Subtract.

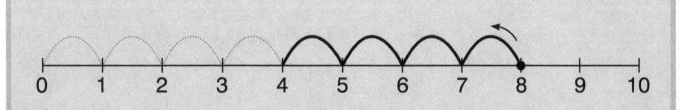

$$8 - 4 = \underline{\quad 4 \quad}$$

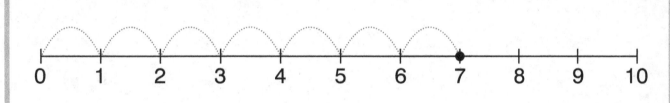

$$7 - 3 = \underline{\qquad}$$

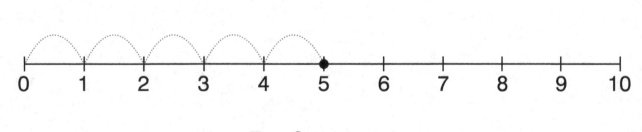

$$5 - 2 = \underline{\qquad}$$

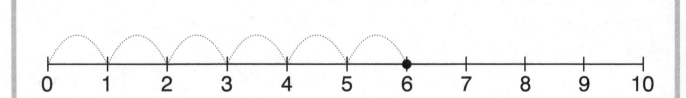

$$6 - 4 = \underline{\qquad}$$

NS1-37 Using Number Lines to Subtract *(continued)*

☐ Show where to start tracing.
☐ Trace 5 leaps back.
☐ Subtract.

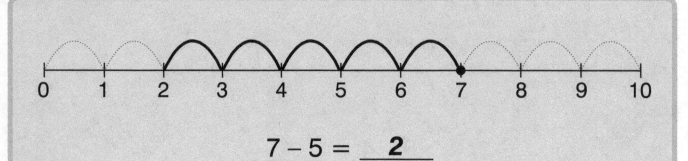

$$7 - 5 = \underline{\quad 2 \quad}$$

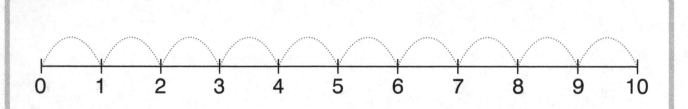

$$9 - 5 = \underline{\qquad}$$

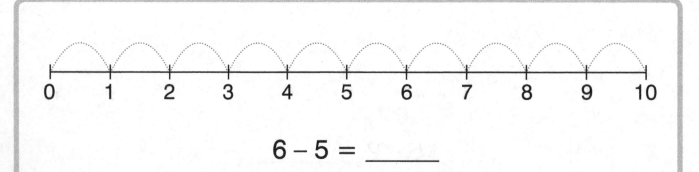

$$6 - 5 = \underline{\qquad}$$

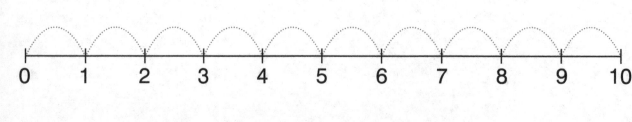

$$10 - 5 = \underline{\qquad}$$

NS1-37 Using Number Lines to Subtract (continued)

☐ Show where to start tracing.
☐ Trace the correct number of leaps back.
☐ Subtract.

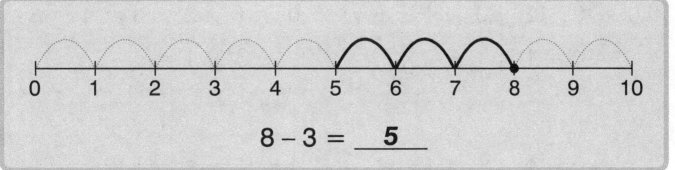

$$8 - 3 = \underline{\ \ 5\ \ }$$

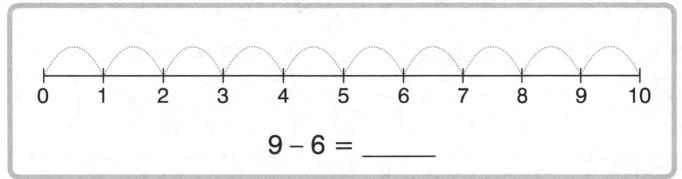

$$9 - 6 = \underline{\hspace{2cm}}$$

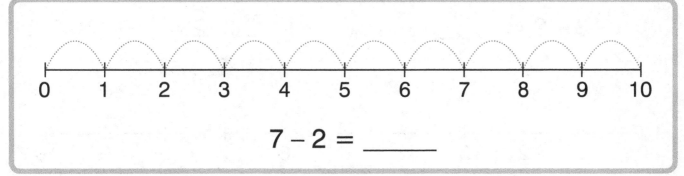

$$7 - 2 = \underline{\hspace{2cm}}$$

☐ Now write the answer on the left.

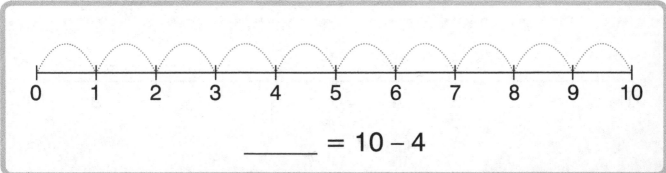

$$\underline{\hspace{2cm}} = 10 - 4$$

NS1-37 Using Number Lines to Subtract (continued)

☐ Add or subtract using the number line.

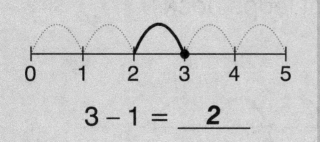

3 − 1 = __2__

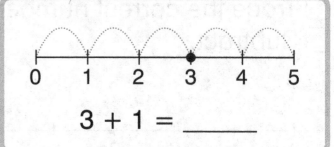

3 + 1 = _____

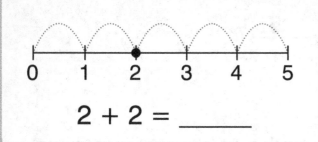

2 + 2 = _____

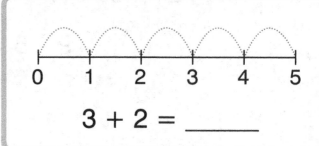

2 − 2 = _____

3 − 2 = _____

3 + 2 = _____

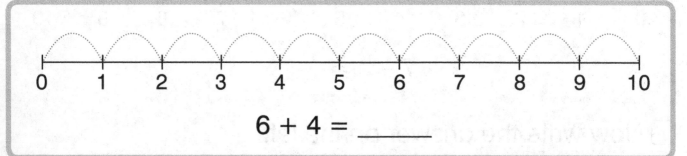

6 + 4 = _____

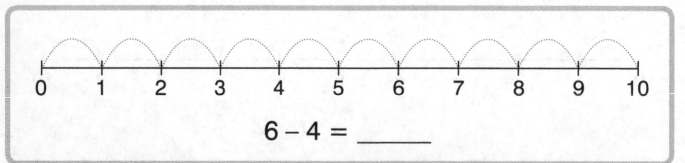

6 − 4 = _____

NS1-38 Counting Back

☐ Write the number that comes **after**.

| 3 _4_ | 4 ___ | 9 ___ | 8 ___ | 2 ___ |

| 1 ___ | 0 ___ | 7 ___ | 5 ___ | 6 ___ |

☐ Write the number that comes **before**.

| _2_ 3 4 5 6 7 8 | __ 4 5 6 7 8 | __ 6 7 8 9 10 |

| __ 2 3 4 | __ 6 7 8 | __ 3 4 | __ 5 6 |

☐ Write the number that comes **after**.
☐ Write the number that comes **before**.

| _7_ 8 _9_ | __ 7 ___ | __ 5 ___ | __ 3 ___ |

| __ 4 ___ | __ 9 ___ | __ 2 ___ | __ 6 ___ |

NS1-38 Counting Back (continued)

☐ Write the number that comes before.

__7__ 8 9	___ 4 5	___ 2 3
___ 18 19	___ 14 15	___ 12 13
___ 28 29	___ 24 25	___ 22 23
___ 26 27	___ 21 22	___ 29 30
___ 33 34	___ 46 47	___ 51 52
___ 30 31	___ 50 51	___ 70 71

NS1-39 Counting Back to Subtract

5   _4_   _3_   5 − 2 = __3__

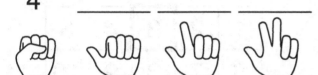

4   _____ _____ _____   4 − 3 = _____

6   _____ _____ _____ _____   6 − 4 = _____

7   _____ _____ _____   7 − 3 = _____

8   _____ _____   8 − 2 = _____

5 − 3 = _____   6 − 3 = _____   7 − 4 = _____

NS1-40 Adding 5 or 10

☐ Shade the next 5 numbers.
☐ Add 5.

1	2	3	**4**	5
6	7	8	9	10

4 + 5 = __9__

1	**2**	3	4	5
6	7	8	9	10

2 + 5 = _____

1	2	3	4	5
6	7	8	9	10

1 + 5 = _____

1	2	**3**	4	5
6	7	8	9	10

3 + 5 = _____

☐ Move down a row to add 5.

1	2	3	**4**	5
6	7	8	9	10

4 + 5 = __9__

5 + 5 = _____

2 + 5 = _____

3 + 5 = _____

1 + 5 = _____

No unauthorized copying

NS1-40 Adding 5 or 10 (continued)

☐ Shade the next 10 numbers.
☐ Add 10.

1	2	3	4	5	6	7	8	9	10
11	12	13	14	15	16	17	18	19	20

4 + 10 = __14__

1	2	3	4	5	6	7	8	9	10
11	12	13	14	15	16	17	18	19	20

9 + 10 = _____

1	2	3	4	5	6	7	8	9	10
11	12	13	14	15	16	17	18	19	20

1 + 10 = _____

1	2	3	4	5	6	7	8	9	10
11	12	13	14	15	16	17	18	19	20

10 + 10 = _____

No unauthorized copying **Number Sense 2**

NS1-40 Adding 5 or 10 (continued)

☐ Move down a row to add 10.

1	2	3	4	5	6	7	8	9	10
11	12	13	14	15	16	17	18	19	20

2 + 10 = ___

7 + 10 = ___

9 + 10 = ___

6 + 10 = ___

1 + 10 = ___

5 + 10 = ___

10 + 10 = ___

8 + 10 = ___

3 + 10 = ___

Bonus: Cover the rest of the page!

7 + 10 = ___

9 + 10 = ___

4 + 10 = ___

NS1-41 Pairs Adding to 5 or 10

3	+	2	=	5
fingers up		fingers not up		altogether

☐ Hold up the correct number of fingers.
  How many are not up?

$$1 + \boxed{} = 5$$

$$4 + \boxed{} = 5$$

$$\begin{array}{r} 2 \\ + \boxed{} \\ \hline 5 \end{array}$$

$$\begin{array}{r} \boxed{} \\ + \ 1 \\ \hline 5 \end{array}$$

$$\begin{array}{r} \boxed{} \\ + \ 3 \\ \hline 5 \end{array}$$

$$\begin{array}{r} 5 \\ + \boxed{} \\ \hline 5 \end{array}$$

$$2 + 3 = \boxed{} + 4 = 3 + \boxed{}$$

Bonus

$$2 + 1 + 2 = 1 + \boxed{} + 1$$

NS1-41 Pairs Adding to 5 or 10 *(continued)*

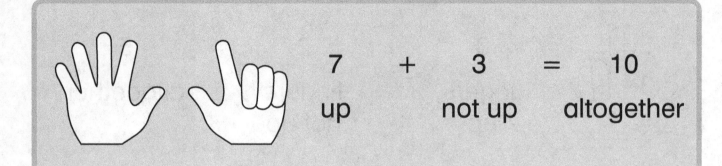

$$7 \quad + \quad 3 \quad = \quad 10$$

up   not up   altogether

☐ Hold up the correct number of fingers.
How many are not up?

$$4 + \boxed{} = 10$$

$$5 + \boxed{} = 10$$

$$\begin{array}{r} 8 \\ + \boxed{} \\ \hline 10 \end{array}$$

$$\begin{array}{r} 3 \\ + \boxed{} \\ \hline 10 \end{array}$$

$$\begin{array}{r} \boxed{} \\ + 9 \\ \hline 10 \end{array}$$

$$\begin{array}{r} 10 \\ + \boxed{} \\ \hline 10 \end{array}$$

$$7 + 3 = \boxed{} + 4 = 8 + \boxed{}$$

Bonus

$$10 = 3 + \boxed{} + 4 = 7 + \boxed{} + 1$$

NS1-42 One More, One Less

$3 + 2 = 5$

so $4 + 2 = \underline{\ \ 6\ \ }$

$7 + 3 = 10$

so $8 + 3 = \underline{\hspace{2cm}}$

$8 + 2 = 10$

so $9 + 2 = \underline{\hspace{2cm}}$

$6 + 4 = 10$

so $6 + 5 = \underline{\hspace{2cm}}$

$4 + 1 = 5$

so $4 + 2 = \underline{\hspace{2cm}}$

$6 + 4 = 10$

so $7 + 4 = \underline{\hspace{2cm}}$

$5 + 6 = \underline{\hspace{2cm}}$

$3 + 3 = \underline{\hspace{2cm}}$

NS1-42 One More, One Less (continued)

7 + 3 = 10   ○○○○○○○ ○○○

so   7 + 2 = __9__   ○○○○○○○ ✗○○

3 + 2 = 5   ○○○ ○○

so   3 + 1 = _____   ○○○ ✗○

6 + 4 = 10   ○○○○○○ ○○○○

so   5 + 4 = _____   ○○○○○✗ ○○○○

4 + 1 = 5   ○○○○ ○

so   4 + 0 = _____   ○○○○ ✗

5 + 5 = 10

so   4 + 5 = _____

2 + 3 = 5

so   2 + 2 = _____

4 + 1 = 5

so   3 + 1 = _____

5 + 5 = 10

so   5 + 4 = _____

NS1-42 One More, One Less (continued)

$6 + 4 = 10$

so $6 + 3 = $ _____

$6 + 4 = 10$

so $5 + 4 = $ _____

$7 + 3 = 10$

so $7 + 4 = $ _____

$7 + 3 = 10$

so $7 + 2 = $ _____

$7 + 3 = 10$

so $6 + 3 = $ _____

$5 + 5 = 10$

so $5 + 6 = $ _____

$5 + 5 = 10$

so $4 + 5 = $ _____

$8 + 3 = $ _____

$2 + 9 = $ _____

No unauthorized copying

NS1-43 Patterns in Adding

☐ Colour the correct number of hearts.
☐ Finish the addition sentence.

0 + **4** = 4   ♥ ♥ ♥ ♥
coloured   not coloured

1 + ☐ = 4   ♥ ♡ ♡ ♡
coloured   not coloured

2 + ☐ = 4   ♡ ♡ ♡ ♡
coloured   not coloured

3 + ☐ = 4   ♡ ♡ ♡ ♡
coloured   not coloured

4 + ☐ = 4   ♡ ♡ ♡ ♡
coloured   not coloured

As the number of ♥ goes up by 1,
the number of ♡ goes _____.

NS1-43 Patterns in Adding (continued)

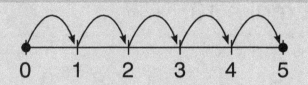

0 + 5 = 5

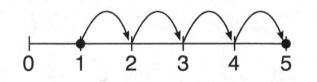

1 + ☐ = ☐

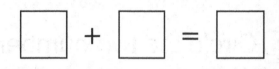

☐ + ☐ = ☐

☐ + ☐ = ☐

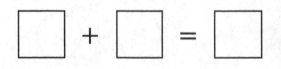

☐ + ☐ = ☐

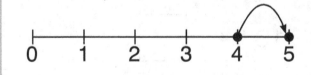

☐ + ☐ = ☐

Which number is the same every time?

1st number   2nd number   total

As the 1st number goes up by 1,

the 2nd number _____.

NS1-44 Using 5 or 10 to Add

☐ Circle the two numbers that make 10.

④ 5 ⑥	3 7 9	1 8 9
4 5 5	2 3 8	3 6 4

☐ Circle the two numbers that make 10.
☐ Write the number that is left over.

⑧ + ② + 5 = 10 + **5**

4 + 6 + 3 = 10 + ☐

2 + 9 + 1 = 10 + ☐

6 + 7 + 4 = 10 + ☐

4 + 3 + 7 = 10 + ☐

NS1-44 Using 5 or 10 to Add (continued)

☐ Circle the two numbers that make 10.
☐ Use 10 to add.

⑧ + 3 + ② = 10 + 3 = 13	2 + 7 + 3 = 10 + ☐ = ☐	1 + 8 + 9 = 10 + ☐ = ☐
3 + 7 + 4 = 10 + ☐ = 13	4 + 5 + 6 = 10 + ☐ = ☐	5 + 5 + 6 = 10 + ☐ = ☐
9 + 2 + 1 = 10 + ☐ = ☐	3 + 2 + 8 = 10 + ☐ = ☐	4 + 5 + 5 = 10 + ☐ = ☐
8 + 4 + 2 = 10 + ☐ = ☐	7 + 3 + 9 = 10 + ☐ = ☐	6 + 4 + 8 = 10 + ☐ = ☐

NS1-45 Number Lines and Number Sentences

☐ Count the leaps.

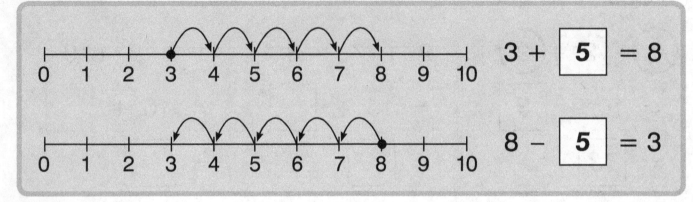

$3 + \boxed{5} = 8$

$8 - \boxed{5} = 3$

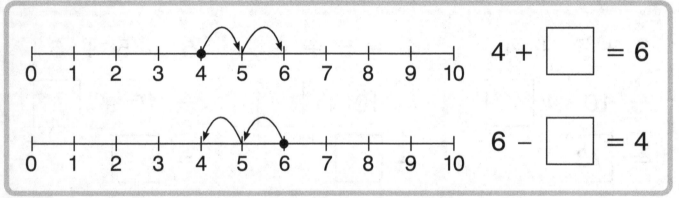

$4 + \boxed{} = 6$

$6 - \boxed{} = 4$

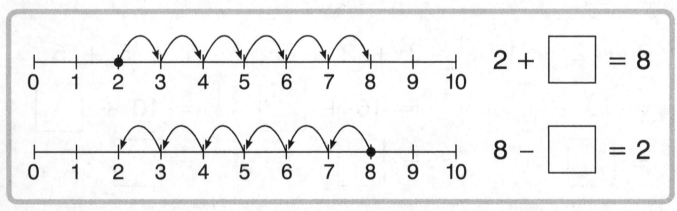

$2 + \boxed{} = 8$

$8 - \boxed{} = 2$

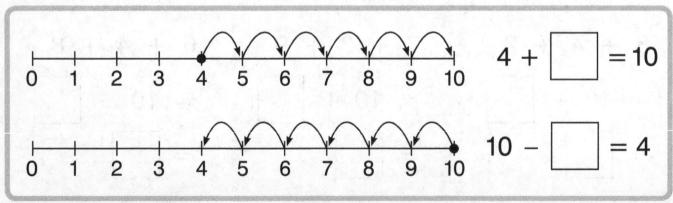

$4 + \boxed{} = 10$

$10 - \boxed{} = 4$

NS1-45 Number Lines and Number Sentences

(continued)

☐ Finish the number sentences.

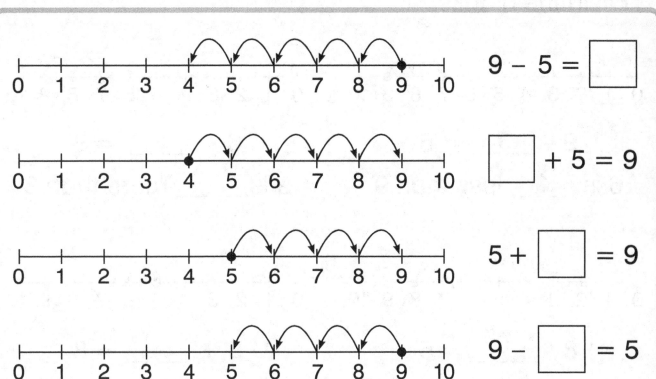

$9 - 5 =$ ☐

☐ $+ 5 = 9$

$5 +$ ☐ $= 9$

$9 -$ ☐ $= 5$

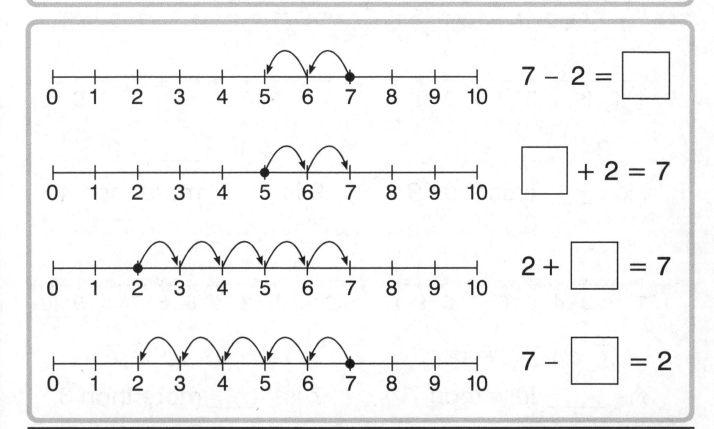

$7 - 2 =$ ☐

☐ $+ 2 = 7$

$2 +$ ☐ $= 7$

$7 -$ ☐ $= 2$

NS1-45 Number Lines and Number Sentences

(continued)

☐ Draw the leaps on the number line.
☐ Fill in the blanks.

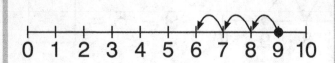

9 – __3__ = 6

6 is __3__ less than 9

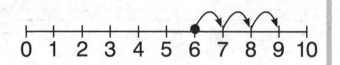

6 + ____ = 9

9 is ____ more than 6

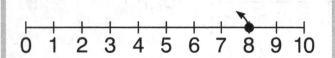

8 – ____ = 5

5 is ____ less than 8

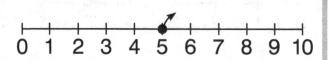

5 + ____ = 8

8 is ____ more than 5

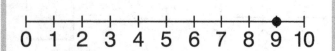

9 – ____ = 4

4 is ____ less than 9

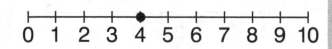

4 + ____ = 9

9 is ____ more than 4

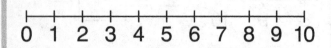

7 – ____ = 3

3 is ____ less than 7

3 + ____ = 7

7 is ____ more than 3

NS1-46 Pictures and Number Sentences

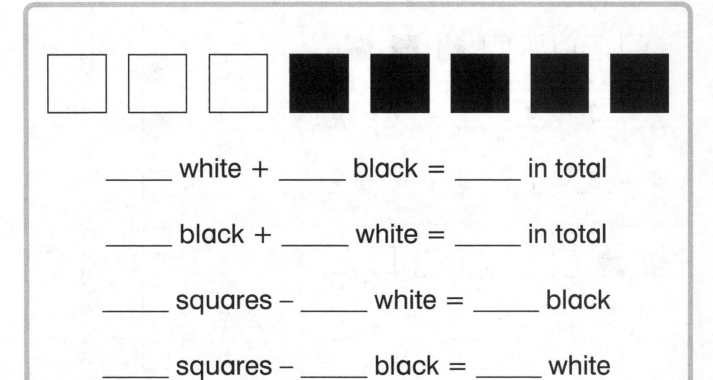

_____ white + _____ black = _____ in total

_____ black + _____ white = _____ in total

_____ squares – _____ white = _____ black

_____ squares – _____ black = _____ white

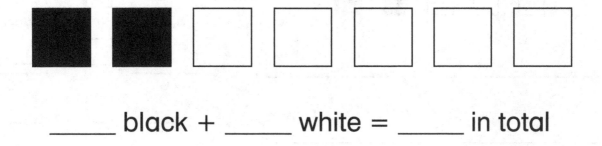

_____ black + _____ white = _____ in total

_____ white + _____ black = _____ in total

_____ squares – _____ white = _____ black

_____ squares – _____ black = _____ white

NS1-46 Pictures and Number Sentences *(cont'd)*

⬚ Write 4 number sentences for each picture.

$\underline{7} - \underline{3} = \underline{4}$ $\underline{7} - \underline{4} = \underline{3}$

$\underline{4} + \underline{3} = \underline{7}$ $\underline{3} + \underline{4} = \underline{7}$

$$\begin{array}{r} 2 \\ + 4 \\ \hline 6 \end{array}$$ ■ $$\begin{array}{r} 6 \\ - 4 \\ \hline 2 \end{array}$$

■

□

□

$$\begin{array}{r} 4 \\ + 2 \\ \hline 6 \end{array}$$ □ $$\begin{array}{r} 6 \\ - 2 \\ \hline 4 \end{array}$$

□

□

$$\underline{\quad} - \underline{\quad} = \underline{\quad} \qquad \underline{\quad} - \underline{\quad} = \underline{\quad}$$

$$\underline{\quad} + \underline{\quad} = \underline{\quad} \qquad \underline{\quad} + \underline{\quad} = \underline{\quad}$$

_____   _____

_____   _____

□

$$\begin{array}{r} \underline{\quad} \\ + \underline{\quad} \\ \hline \underline{\quad} \end{array}$$ □ $$\begin{array}{r} \underline{\quad} \\ - \underline{\quad} \\ \hline \underline{\quad} \end{array}$$

□

□

$$\begin{array}{r} \underline{\quad} \\ + \underline{\quad} \\ \hline \underline{\quad} \end{array}$$ □ $$\begin{array}{r} \underline{\quad} \\ - \underline{\quad} \\ \hline \underline{\quad} \end{array}$$

■

_____   _____

_____   _____

NS1-46 **Pictures and Number Sentences** *(cont'd)*

☐ Write 4 number sentences for each picture.

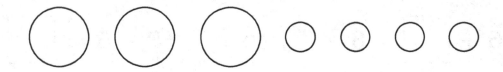

Bonus: Write 8 number sentences.

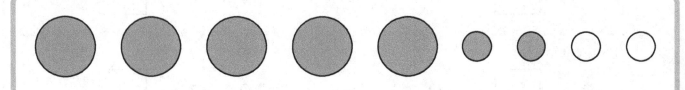

NS1-47 Counting Forwards to Subtract

☐ Subtract by counting forwards.

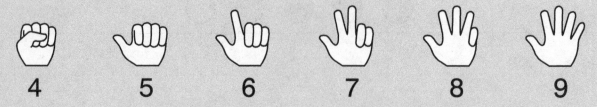

| 4 | 5 | 6 | 7 | 8 | 9 |

4 + | 5 | = 9   so   9 – 4 = | 5 |

6 + | | = 8   so   8 – 6 = | |

8 + | | = 9   so   9 – 8 = | |

3 + | | = 8   so   8 – 3 = | |

7 + | | = 10   so   10 – 7 = | |

9 – 5 = | | 10 – 5 = | |

8 – 4 = | | 7 – 2 = | |

NS1-48 Skip Counting by 2s

☐ Start at 2 and count by 2s.
☐ Colour the numbers that you say.

1	2	3	4	5	6	7	8	9	10
11	12	13	14	15	16	17	18	19	20
21	22	23	24	25	26	27	28	29	30

☐ Use the number line to count by 2s.

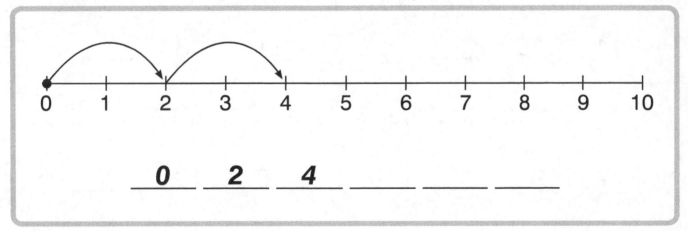

_0_ _2_ _4_ ____ ____ ____

☐ Fill in the blanks.

2, 4, ____, ____, 10,

12, 14, 16, ____, 20,

22, ____, ____, 28, 30.

NS1-48 Skip Counting by 2s (continued)

☐ Start at 1 and count by 2s.
☐ Colour the numbers that you say.

1	2	3	4	5	6	7	8	9	10
11	12	13	14	15	16	17	18	19	20
21	22	23	24	25	26	27	28	29	30

☐ Find the missing number.

14   16   _____   11   13   _____

7   9   _____   8   10   _____

10   _____   14   16   _____   20

15   _____   19   9   _____   13

No unauthorized copying

NS1-49 Grouping to Count

How many?

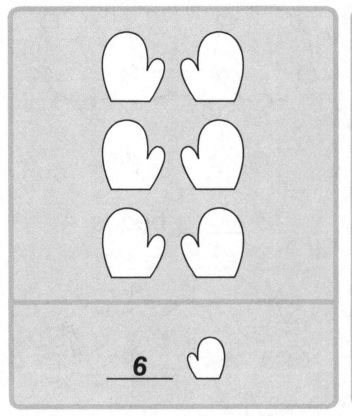

6

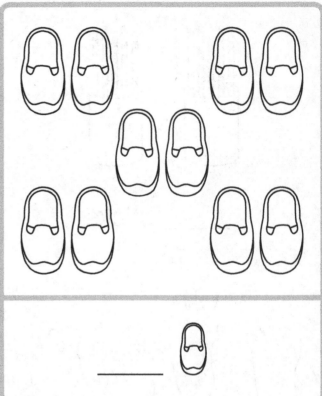

_____

_____

NS1-49 **Grouping to Count** (continued)

How many?

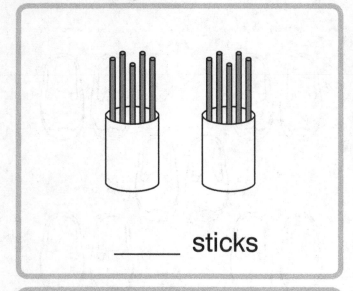

_____ sticks

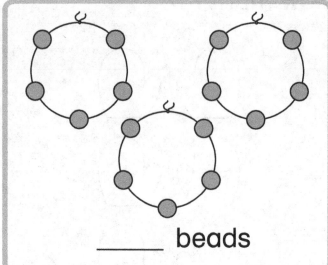

_____ beads

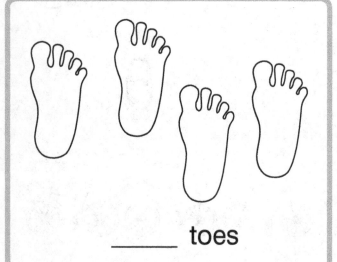

_____ toes

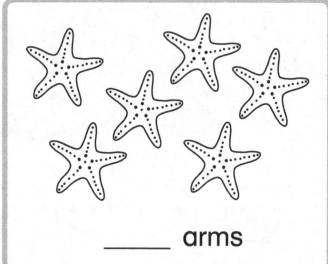

_____ arms

_____ birds

No unauthorized copying

JUMP AT HOME GRADE 1

NS1-49 **Grouping to Count** (continued)

☐ Count by 5s and then by 1s to see how many.

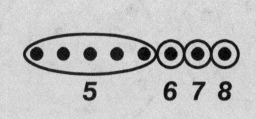

5 6 7 8

___8___

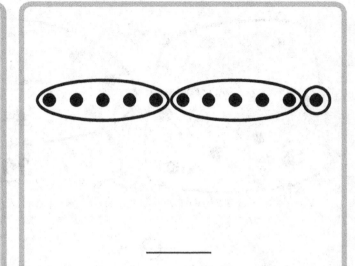

_____

_____

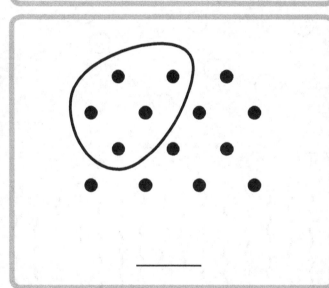

_____

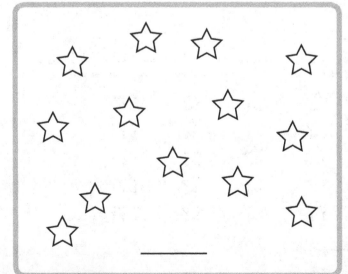

_____

_____

NS1-49 Grouping to Count (continued)

☐ Group by 10s to see how many.

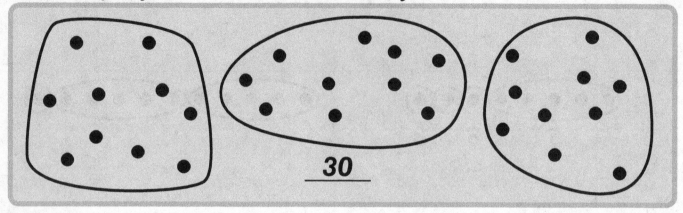

_30_

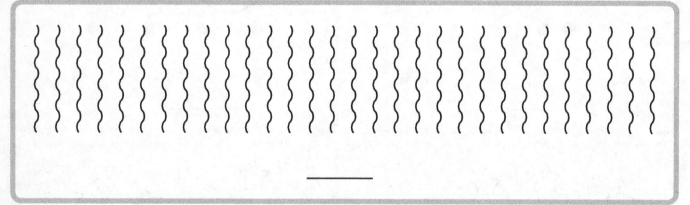

_____

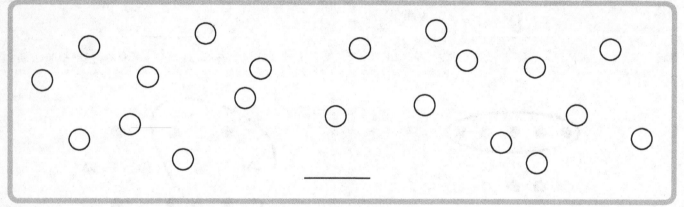

_____

_____

NS1-50 Grouping to Estimate

☐ Estimate how many dots.
☐ Count by grouping 10s.

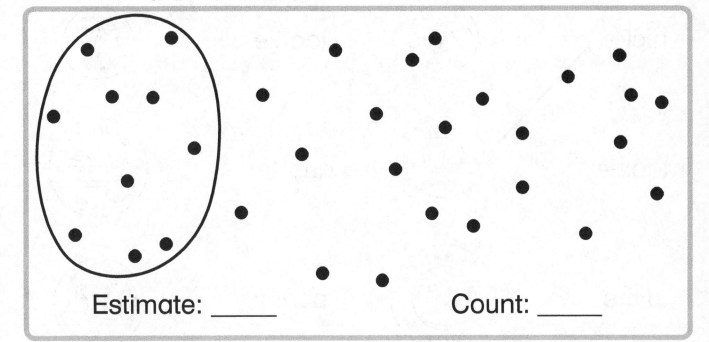

Estimate: _____   Count: _____

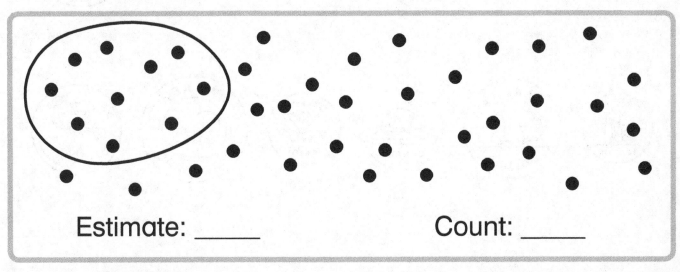

Estimate: _____   Count: _____

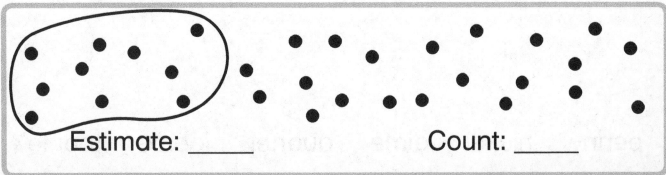

Estimate: _____   Count: _____

NS1-51 Identifying Coins

☐ Match each coin with its picture.

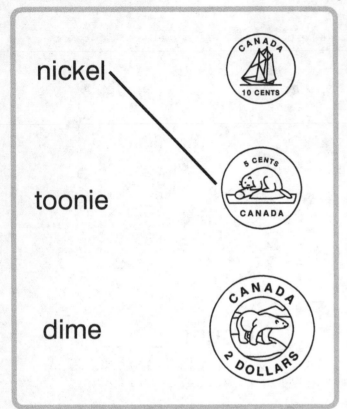

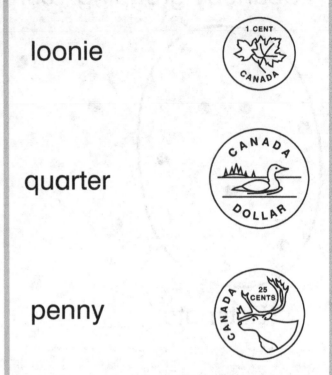

penny   nickel   dime   quarter   loonie   toonie

NS1-52 Coin Values

☐ Write the value on the coin.

NS1-53 How Much Money?

☐ Write how much.

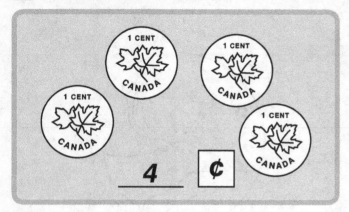

4 ¢

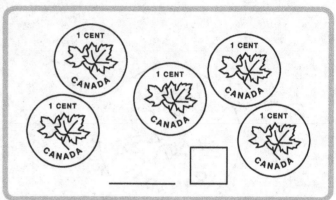

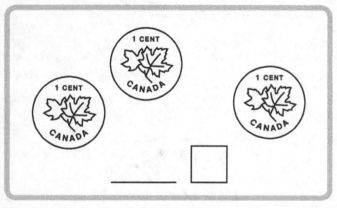

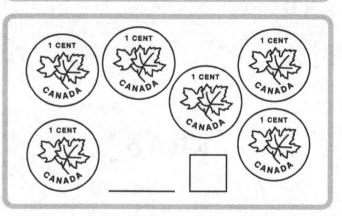

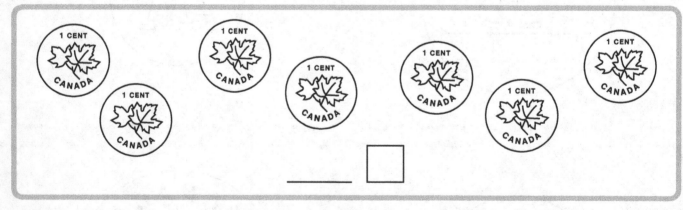

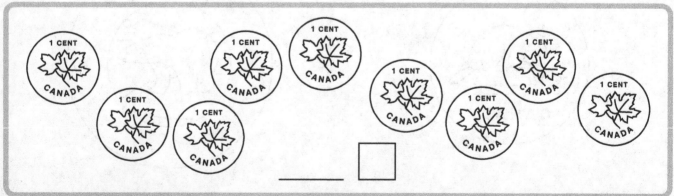

UNIT 6

Patterns and Algebra 2

PA1-6 Two Ways to Find the Same Total

☐ Count the shaded squares in each **row**.
☐ Write an addition sentence for the total number
of shaded squares.

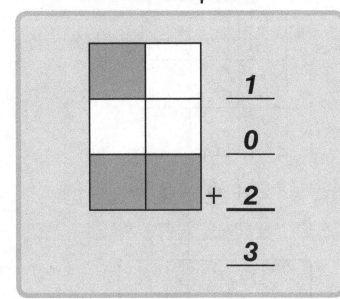

$\underline{\ \ 1\ \ }$

$\underline{\ \ 0\ \ }$

$+\underline{\ \ 2\ \ }$

$\underline{\ \ 3\ \ }$

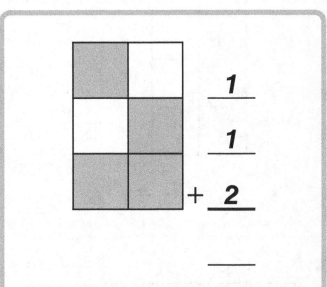

$\underline{\ \ 1\ \ }$

$\underline{\ \ 1\ \ }$

$+\underline{\ \ 2\ \ }$

$\underline{\ \ \ \ \ }$

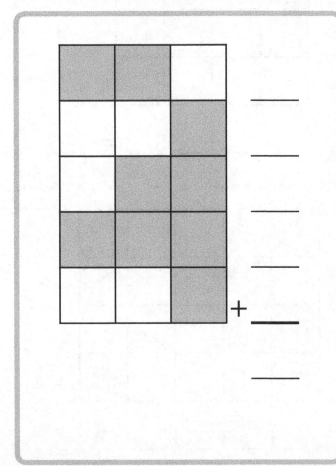

$\underline{\ \ \ \ \ }$

$\underline{\ \ \ \ \ }$

$\underline{\ \ \ \ \ }$

$\underline{\ \ \ \ \ }$

$+\underline{\ \ \ \ \ }$

$\underline{\ \ \ \ \ }$

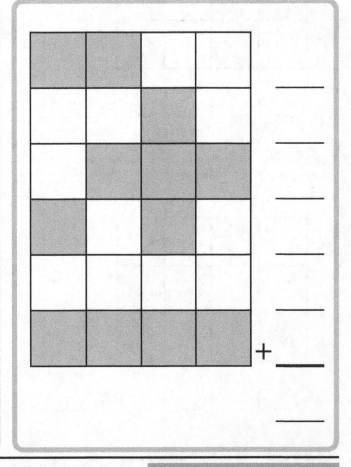

$\underline{\ \ \ \ \ }$

$\underline{\ \ \ \ \ }$

$\underline{\ \ \ \ \ }$

$\underline{\ \ \ \ \ }$

$\underline{\ \ \ \ \ }$

$+\underline{\ \ \ \ \ }$

$\underline{\ \ \ \ \ }$

PA1-6 Two Ways to Find the Same Total *(cont'd)*

☐ Count the shaded squares in each **column**.
☐ Write an addition sentence for the total number
   of shaded squares.

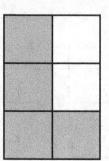

___+ **1** = ___

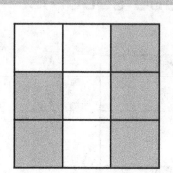

2 + **0** + **3** = ___

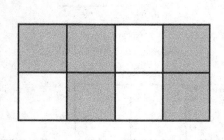

___+___+___+___ = ___

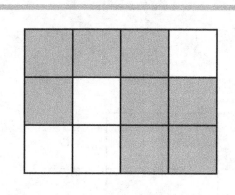

___+___+___+___ = ___

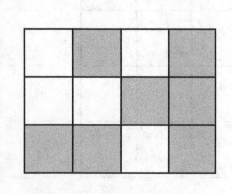

___+___+___+___ = ___

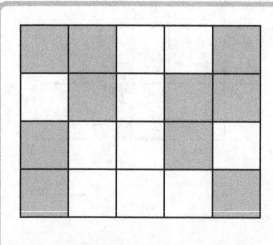

___+___+___+___+___=___

PA1-6 Two Ways to Find the Same Total *(cont'd)*

☐ Write 2 addition sentences for the total number
of shaded squares.

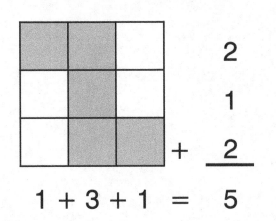

2

1

+ __2__

1 + 3 + 1 = 5

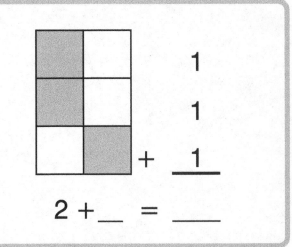

1

1

+ __1__

2 + __ = ___

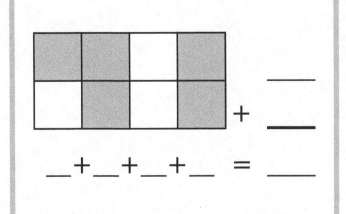

+ _____

__ + __ + __ + __ = ___

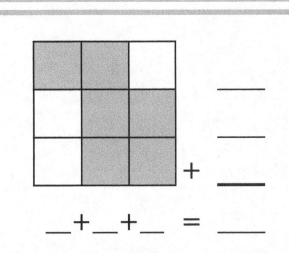

___

___

+ _____

__ + __ + __ = ___

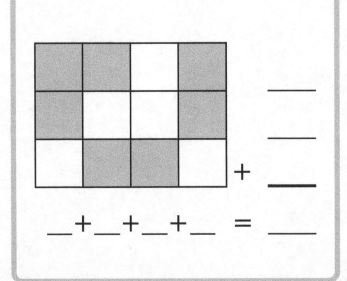

___

___

+ _____

__ + __ + __ + __ = ___

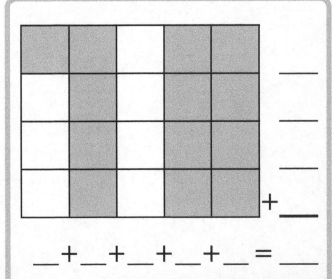

___

___

___

___

+ _____

__ + __ + __ + __ + __ = ___

UNIT 7

Measurement 2

ME1-4 Clock Faces

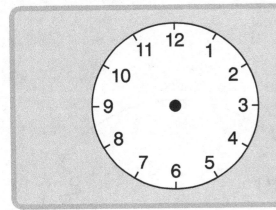

This is a clock face.

Numbers start at 1 and end at 12.

☐ Fill in the missing 3, 6, 9, or 12.

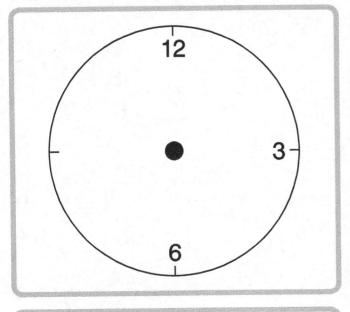

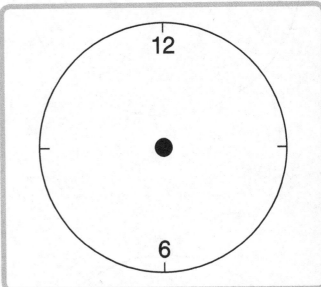

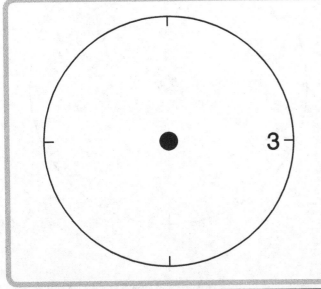

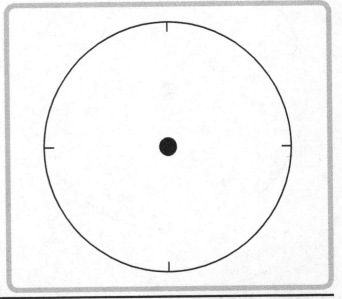

ME1-4 Clock Faces (continued)

☐ Fill in the missing numbers.

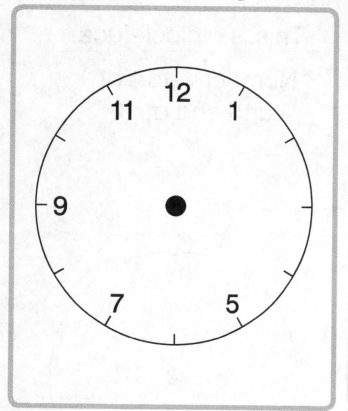

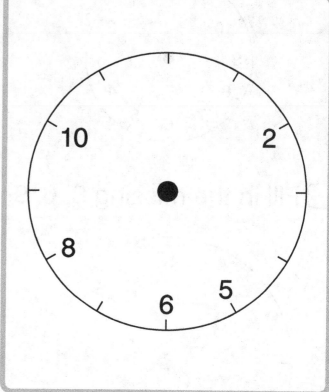

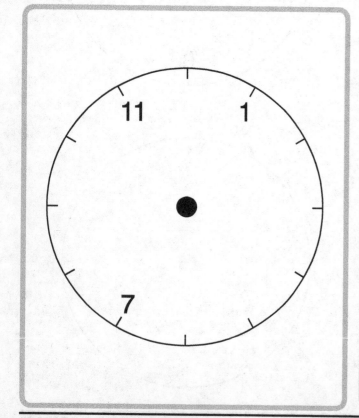

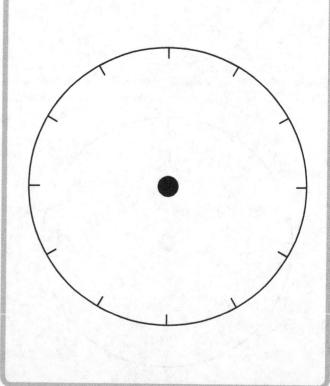

No unauthorized copying

ME1-5 The Hour Hand

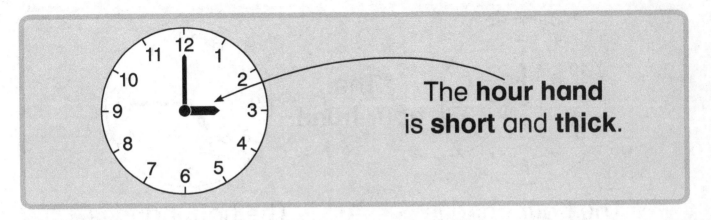

The **hour hand** is **short** and **thick**.

☐ Circle the hour hand.

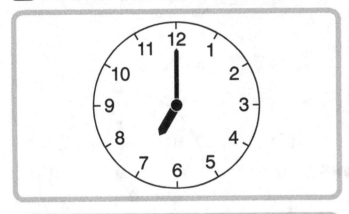

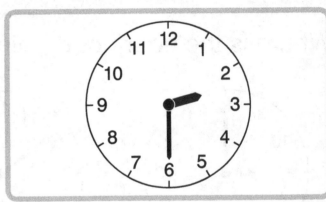

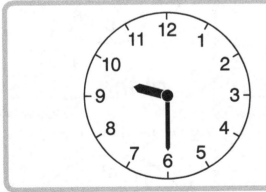

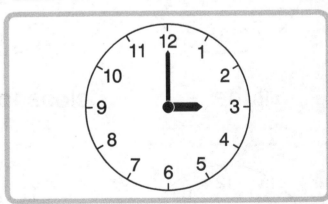

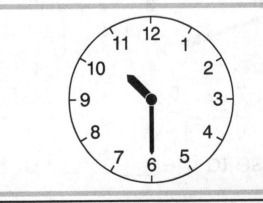

ME1-5 The Hour Hand (continued)

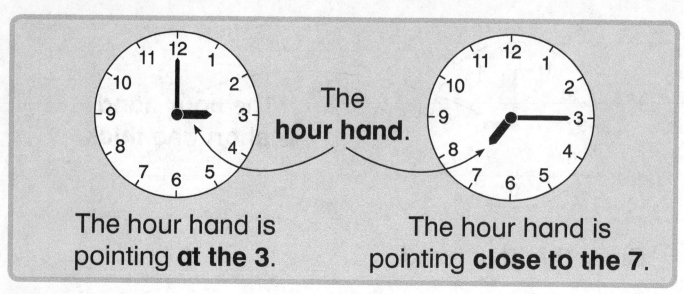

The **hour hand**.

The hour hand is pointing **at the 3**.

The hour hand is pointing **close to the 7**.

Where is the hour hand pointing?

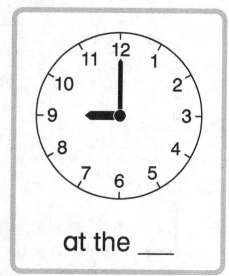

at the ___

close to the ___

at the ___

close to the ___

at the ___

close to the ___

ME1-6 Time to the Hour

 It is **9 o'clock.**

☐ Write the time shown on each clock.

 _____ o'clock

 _____ o'clock

 _____ o'clock

 _____

 _____

 _____

 _____

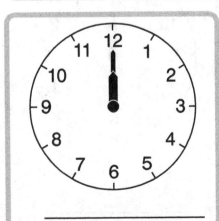 _____

 _____

ME1-6 Time to the Hour (continued)

☐ Write the time in two ways.

6 o'clock

6 :00

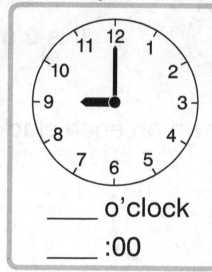

____ o'clock

____ :00

____ o'clock

____ :00

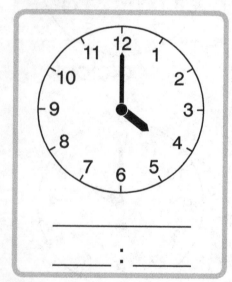

_____

____ : ____

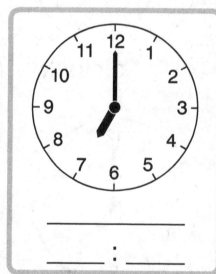

_____

____ : ____

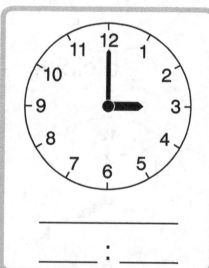

_____

____ : ____

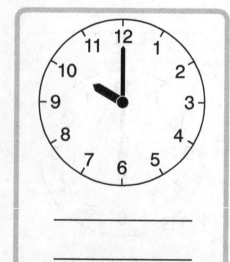

_____

_____

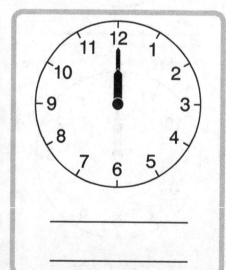

_____

_____

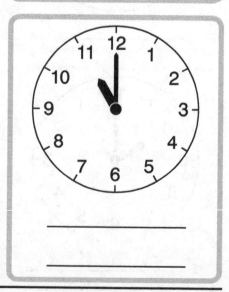

_____

_____

ME1-7 Time to the Half Hour

It is **half past 3**.

☐ Write the time.

half past _____

half past _____

half past _____

_____

_____

_____

_____

_____

_____

ME1-7 Time to the Half Hour *(continued)*

☐ Write the time in two ways.

half past __3__

__3__ : __30__

half past ____

____ : 30

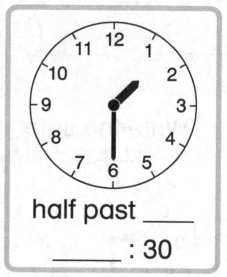

half past ____

____ : 30

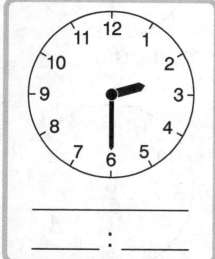

____
____ : ____

____
____ : ____

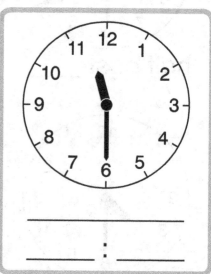

____
____ : ____

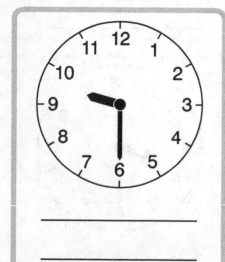

____
____

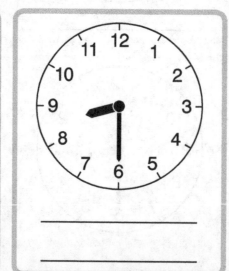

____
____

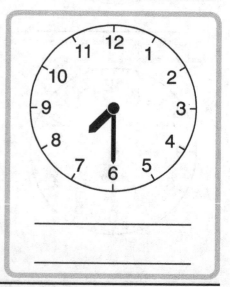

____
____

ME1-7 Time to the Half Hour (continued)

☐ Match the analogue clocks to the digital clocks.

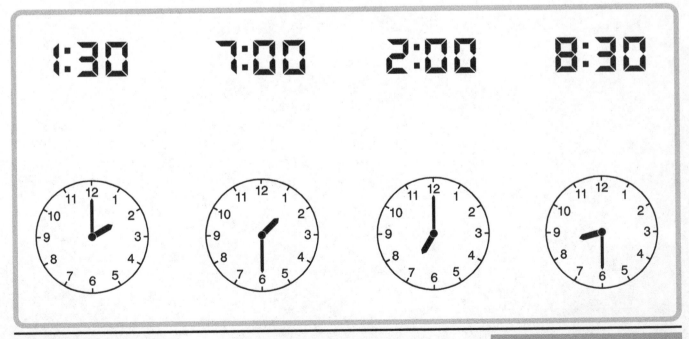

No unauthorized copying

About the Authors

JOHN MIGHTON is a mathematician, author, and playwright. He completed a Ph.D. in mathematics at the University of Toronto and is currently a fellow of the Fields Institute for Mathematical Research. The founder of JUMP Math (www.jumpmath.org), Mighton also gives lectures to student teachers at York University and the Ontario Institute for Studies in Education, and invited talks and training sessions for parents and educators. He is the author of the *JUMP at Home* workbooks and the national bestsellers *The Myth of Ability* and *The End of Ignorance*. He has won the Governor General's Literary Award and the Siminovitch Prize for his plays.

DR. ANNA KLEBANOV received her B.Sc., M.Sc., Ph.D., and teaching certificate from the Technion – Israel Institute of Technology. She is the recipient of three teaching awards for excellence. She began her career at JUMP Math as a curriculum writer in 2007, working with Dr. John Mighton and Dr. Sindi Sabourin on JUMP Math's broad range of publications.

DR. SINDI SABOURIN received her Ph.D. in mathematics from Queen's University, specializing in commutative algebra. She is the recipient of the Governor General's Gold Medal Award from Queen's University and a National Sciences and Research Council Postdoctoral Fellowship. Her career with JUMP Math began in 2003 as a volunteer doing in-class tutoring and one-on-one tutoring, as well as working on answer keys. In 2006, she became a curriculum writer working on JUMP Math's broad range of publications.